CASH IN!

Be more wealthy!
A bottoms-up practical view of money and people
in poverty, commerce, finance, and power.

Author: Manny Perez (Manuel F Perez), MPA, CAMS

Second Edition, it is an expanded presentation of "Three Monetary Ecosystems" by the same author.

CreateSpace Edition

ISBN-13: 978-1974558308

ISBN-13: 978-1974558308
Imprint: Independently published

Published with the assistance of CENACI and Fondo Editorial Científico, Caracas, Venezuela and Coach Hispano of NYC, USA

NYC, Sept., 2017

<u>Disclaimer:</u> This work is the product of grass roots observation, experience and analysis. The author is not an economist nor a monetary specialist, just a renaissance man, a free thinker who has lived overseas and worked in non-profit, private, public and commercial sectors, including prevention of money laundering, surviving triple digit inflation and devaluation, losing everything a number of times, and managing to be successful and prosperous in spite of it all. For this reason, **nothing in this book should be considered a recommendation to invest or divest or to make financial decisions of any kind.** The chapter and comments on cashing in reflect life lessons and must be weighed against the reader's own experiences and reality.

Table of Contents

ABOUT THE AUTHOR 6

THANK YOU 9

INTRODUCTION 10

PREFACE 17

I.   Commerce and Payments: The First Ecosystem 22

    Barter 22

    Exchange - The Origins of Money...................................23

    Money and Commerce...24

    The Need for Money 25

    Creating the idea of Wealth 26

    The Free Market that Isn't 32

    The Birth of International Markets 34

    Warfare and Economic Value..37

    Collaborative International Commerce.........................42

    A special note for traditional economics thinkers: 44

II.   Banking and Finance – the Second Ecosystem **46**

    The Effect of greater International Trade 49

    The expansion of Banking 52

    The use of Corporations for Creating wealth 56

    20th Century Global Financial System 57

    The need for Government Control................................59

Storing and Exchanging Value with Stocks and Commodities 62

Money Service Businesses 63

III. Government and Power Transactions – the Third Ecosystem 66

Monetary Supply in the British American Colonies 67

Fiat and the Principle of Scarce Resources 68

Politics and the Principle of Fiat 72

The Principle of Forgetfulness 76

Government Transactions with Constituents 79

IV. Wealth Accrual and Control 84

Wealth Accrual 84

Wealth Control 86

Effects of Concentrating Wealth 88

Adding Value To Wealth: Government protections 89

    Monetary Deposits 91

    Secured Investment 92

Creating Wealth and Value 93

Payment Systems 93

Debt 94

Deferred Payments 95

Legally binding promises to Pay 96

Credit 96

Stock Market 97

Commodities Markets 98

Consumer Financial Services 99

Global Foreign Exchange 99

Collateral – High Quality Assets 100

Is Money still a Measure of Wealth? 101

Regional and Global Wealth Creation 107

V. Integrating the Three Ecosystems 112

Why speak of Ecosystems? 113

Money Laundering and Corruption 116

Criminal Wealth 117

The Unbanked and Cryptocurrency 119

VI. Cash In 124

Payments and Commerce Ecosystem: 127

The Banking and Finance Ecosystem 130

The Government (Governance) and Power Monetary Ecosystem 135

CASH IN on good advice! 146

VI. Conclusion 148

Bibliography 152

    T. Harv Eker "Secrets of the Millionaire Mind" 152

    Other sources 153

Special Drawing Rights and the International Monetary Fund 154

ABOUT THE AUTHOR

Manny Perez (Manuel F. Perez) defines himself as a Renaissance man dedicated to success, learning, helping others, and "being part of the solution".

He holds a Master in Public Administration from New York University, and is a Certified Anti-Money Laundering Specialist. He is also a father of four and a man of family, music, church and community. However, one thing he is not is an economist. In college, he concluded that the only really reliable concept in all of the economics program of his time was "The Pareto Principle" and since then he has been defining economists with the old joke: *an economist is he who spends years preparing a prediction on what will happen, and then spends many more years explaining why his prediction did not come true.*

Though he has met excellent thinkers who are economists, he personally believes far too many government and college economists disregard reality and the social constructs people build, and that these individuals often follow theories that are only partially valid. Realizing that mankind is now in the midst of a new renaissance period, in which we are redefining many of our society's foundations, Manuel decided to write his book on the 3 Monetary Ecosystems that make up Earth's global economy at this time, recognizing that two of these ecosystems are presently being transformed by the renaissance we are undergoing. For this reason, he does not aim to correlate the text to any of the past economic schools of thought or theories, not even Adam Smith's *Wealth of Nations*. He does, though, believe that any economic theory based on scarcity of goods tends to fail once removed from the context of a small, limited community, and so prepared this second edition titles "CASH IN!" for people to consider how to create more riches in each of the systems.

Born in Venezuela, South America, he has been active in NY and Venezuelan local organizations, international Oil Operations, finance, cryptocurrency, empowerment, volunteering, inclusion, civil rights, local and government development, technology, space development policy issues, and non-profits, to name just a few areas of interest. As a Renaissance man, he is known to stand up for his various communities, and works from within corporate and government structures to achieve change. In addition, as an immigrant to the USA he understands the personal and shared problems of the people he represents as an elected member of the New York State Democratic Committee.

An international entrepreneur and business promoter, as well as a certified master coach, he loves helping others reach success, and hopes this work will help some entrepreneurs avoid some of the logical traps that many of them fall into when dealing with the truisms of Western Civilization's market economy and financial services. He is author of various titles in English and Spanish, including "Creating Volunteers" and "Using The Great Within".

THANK YOU

My thanks to everyone who listened to me and gave me hints as to how best to frame my concepts and ideas, and most especially to PhD candidate Ginevra Autino, who edited my draft and found errors and inconsistencies, and Dr. Marielvi Pinero, PhD, who wrote the introduction and was instrumental in framing the specific content for this edition.

Of course, I must mention my wife, Lucia Africano, whose patience with my musings and writing made this text possible, my coach Sandra Macis, who always knew what to say when I was wavering in the midst of writer's block,

For this second edition I also have to thank Tony Severo, of Catholic Charities in NYC, and the many people who read the first edition of the book and suggested small adjustments and a new title and chapter, focusing on a practical benefit for the reader.

Finally, I wish to thank all the authors that gave me insights and explanations that allowed me to put these pages together, as well as the source of all inspiration, my inner self and my Creator (under whatever name you wish to use).

Manuel Perez, MPA, CAMS

INTRODUCTION

Money is nothing but a tool and a human construct, and it has been available—in one form or another—to most people in the 21st century via the 3 ecosystems described in these pages. Understanding how money works in each system makes it possible to cash in where others might make avoidable mistakes, resulting in the creation of wealth in new and unexpected ways.

The Payment and Commerce ecosystem, which he considers fundamental to the concept of tangible value, includes interrelationships with buyers, sellers, merchants, consumers, products, property, money, payment technology and more. And he points out that the monetary ecosystems are surrounded by national, regional and global political and economic regulations, which in turn are impacted by technological progress, human power struggles and communications.

He also summarizes that every monetary ecosystem is composed of human beings, and a medium of exchange that allows the acquisition of products and services to meet our needs, generate our own wealth (and the country's), and build better societies.

This book explains simply and with great sense, the evolution of monetary systems. Initially, the author speaks of three ecosystems as a spinning of the elements that arise through time, and after that he explains the creation of wealth and value, which leads to his conclusions.

As an example, within the aspects of the financial ecosystem, the legal framework and economic actors are described, including the subtlety of interrelation with technological changes, and with the inclusion of basic economic and monetary terms necessary for a common individual (who is interested in knowing how) to manage their money. The text encourages that very individual to know the past and learn historical trends in order to understand what is happening to their money, country and the economy as a whole in the present.

The first ecosystem, Payments and Commerce, began with exchange and barter, creating the perspective that all we really need as individuals is to satisfy our own needs, either by exchanging things or through the use of currency (aside from the use of coercion). But, we are not only individuals: we are also groups of individuals organized in communities, in countries. As a consequence, a second ecosystem evolved out of the first: the banking/financial ecosystem, with key actors that include buyers, sellers, merchants, governments and wealthy individuals. Out of necessity, governments and wealthy individuals became the providers or suppliers of money and other financial services. Governments held the power of life and death over their subjects. They also had the control of national treasury, which made them key players in establishing the supply of money for their country and local commerce. However, wealthy individuals could influence government representatives and also increase or decrease money supply if they wished to do so, which they often did.

Government control of money supply was necessary to avoid economic turmoil and manipulation, and it became more difficult as the banking/financial sector grew, so the Third Ecosystem, the Government Transaction Ecosystem, evolved and is still evolving. In this system, individual commercial transactions are almost invisible and seemingly unimportant because key players in this ecosystem basically include: government leaders, Finance Ministers, and other gatekeepers for monetary policies, legislators, central banks, and the news media. Though every country will have a slightly different group participating in this new ecosystem (the third ecosystem), the concept is that they all use monetary policy and government funds to negotiate and exert power and control.

It is interesting to look at this evolutionary process and compare it to that of environmental ecosystems because, all natural ecosystems develop self-regulating feedback loops to protect themselves against one organism or factor destroying everything. It would seem that the desire of the ecosystem itself to survive and grow more balanced over time, implies that human ecosystems would tend to be stable and unchangeable, but history (and Mr. Perez say the contrary: human beings proclaim the benefits of stability and permanence until they do what humans do best by changing the rules and transforming their environment in surprising ways. The history of monetary systems demonstrates that this is so, in spite of the wishes and efforts of governments and the wealthy to maintain stability.

The 20th Century transformation of banking and financial services, and the creation of a global system for controlling transactions, has been an example of this tendency. The creation of fiat currency, combined with central bank and government transactions to manipulate currency value and controls, was yet another transformation. These two changes occurred almost simultaneously, because each depends on the other for its existence. As a consequence, the Commerce/Payment ecosystem was also transformed.

To understand this third ecosystem is key to national wealth accrual because government control allows the calculation and management of the nation's wealth; whether it generates trust or chaos; balances out inequities; freedom or dependence; monetary criminal abuse or ethical behavior that allows for the accumulation of social capital, too.

After explaining the three ecosystems, Mr. Perez writes how in the financial industry many innovations have resulted in new products and additional controls over wealth generation. This industry has grown in leaps and bounds, creating stock markets, payment systems, personal checks, traveler's checks, credit cards, debit cards and electronic transfers, just to mention a few innovations. Further, they have used debt and risk management, stock investment strategies, deferred payments and other financial instruments to stimulate commerce throughout their areas of influence. Without a doubt, technology, especially information and communications technology, has revolutionized these markets and ecosystem, but beyond the benefits to consumers, social problems have arisen that the government must control and resolve somehow.

Mr. Perez also mentions modern developments that are generating much wealth in the Commerce/Payment Ecosystem. One is network marketing, which has resulted in the need for government control and regulation, similar to those over the financial ecosystem. Another important innovation, proposed in 2009 by Satoshi Nakamoto (pseudonym) is a new monetary unit and electronic means of controlling it, called cryptocurrency and popularized with Bitcoin, Ethereum, the Blockchain, and other variations. In Nakamoto's vision, the Financial/Banking ecosystem could be replaced by technology; though it is Perez's opinion that human beings will always want to deal with other humans for some of the services offered in through banking and financial services. Mr. Perez also tells us that the initial invention of Bitcoin (a form of cryptocurrency) and the Blockchain software technology that ensured Bitcoin's security and functionality, which is characterized as a public yet secure distributed ledger, which was declared "open-source" so anyone could share it and improve on the idea. Nevertheless, Mr. Perez points out that cryptocurrency is of limited use when we consider the huge volume of transactions and value that flow daily through each of the three ecosystems. Apparently, it holds promise, but needs to mature before the innovations can make an impact—good or bad—on the ecosystems themselves.

Obviously, cryptocurrency will result in deep changes for people, organizations and required skills for workers, sweeping away with existing habits, lifestyles and shared expectations related to money. It could even lead to violent transformations and adjustments in existing financial markets, as speculators and criminals abuse it before governments can establish proper controls to protect users and investors alike.

And in the "Cash In" chapter, he explains basic principles that apply to each of the ecosystems, with a warning that ignorance can be disastrous in both the banking and financial, and the government and power ecosystems, since both deal with information, communication and knowledge.

The future is clear: a new ecosystem is emerging. It is predicted that 70% of the world's population will use a smartphone or handheld device, including the poor and those with no bank accounts. This implies changes in transactions, in regulations, and in international trade. A new infrastructure will have appeared, new millionaires, and a new way of doing things with new technologies will have become "common sense". Yet there is still something crucial that must be done: the systematic articulation of the new regulatory framework and the appropriate institutions that may be capable of facilitating the functioning of the new economy in a socially and economically sustainable manner in the coming decades.

Manuel Perez has simply managed to summarize the monetary system, for ordinary people who, every day, seek the exchange of products and services to meet their needs, and to create and increase wealth. It is an economics book for non-economists.

Understanding the evolution from barter to virtual currency makes this book an amazing reading experience: Exchange, the origin of money, money and commerce, creating wealth, the free market that isn´t, the birth of international markets, warfare and economic value, collaborative International commerce, international trade, the world of Banking, government controls, are just a few topics that I found fascinating. I have enjoyed it very much and I invite you to add this book to your reading list and enjoy the later reflections on the content and the motivation to consider the subject more closely.

As a non-economist of this world I thank Manuel (Manny) Perez who invited me to write the introduction to his book "Three Monetary Ecosystems". His contribution will, undoubtedly, be of great help with basic concepts of financial knowledge and management that are needed for us to understand the importance and evolution of the monetary system. In summary, "Economics for non-economists" is a concept that has come of age and we can all read it now.

Thanks, Manuel Perez

Marielvi Piñero, PhD, MBA, Ind. Engineer

Professor of Executive Education at School of Management "Instituto de Estudios Superiores de Administración (IESA)" Caracas, Venezuela International Management Consultant in Strategy and Operations.

PREFACE

People like food, and people like money. We actually learn what food we like and the type of money we believe in, and how to benefit from both. But few of us learn how to make our food or money, though having more of either is considered a measure of success (and survival). But, just as we rarely wonder where our food comes from, we rarely wonder where our money comes from: most of us treat money like a form of food and we don't look beyond where we get it, and gladly accept other people's instructions and opinions about where and how to get more. And when these individuals run out of food, or money, they often try to obtain some through any means possible, including destructive behavior or begging for it. Luckily, modern Western societies have greatly reduced the presence of extreme hunger and poverty in their lands, but in some places it is still a reality. Many people believe that in order to get money all they need is a job, that there are plenty of low-skill jobs available (unless they are looking for a job themselves), and that it is impossible to survive without money. But this is not quite true: as we will see later, **money is nothing but a tool and a human construct**, and it is available—in one form or another—to most people in the 21st century via the 3 ecosystems described in these pages.

The purpose of the book is for you to figure out how to CASH IN!

Be aware that most of what you have learned about money and economics actually comes from marketing and government communications, which focus on scarcity and competition, and make you want and do things that you really have no reason to want or do. Those teachings are often wrong, just as economic predictions are often wrong, yet they still ring true to us because they resonate with our personal money experiences, which include:

- What we have in our pockets and wallets must be worth something, because it cost us (unless it's a credit card);
- "money doesn't grow on trees" (but the paper it's printed on is);
- When we spend our money we need to get more (unless you are the government or a bank);
- It takes effort to get money (unless you are born rich).

Of course, these beliefs and the trust in our money can be, and has been, lost when people find that they simply can't buy anything with their money—which can be expected with paper money after, for example, losing a war. This lack of trust in paper money is the reason why many people prefer "coin", jewels, or precious metals. When money is not based on precious metals made into coins, this lack of trust can destroy a country's economy by drastically reducing the amount of money available for commerce, and can destroy a country's wealth by taking away all of the value in the bank accounts belonging to both people and businesses.

Instead, what if what we knew about money were simply about currency exchange between people? Of paying, buying, receiving and giving, all according to ancient barter and haggling traditions? As *Rich Dad, Poor Dad* author Robert Kiyosaki clearly points out, we need to think differently if we want to reach greater wealth.

CASH IN!

This is simply because there is an entire other level to money, one that is fed by banks and financial systems, which goes beyond simple commerce and delves into capital and the wealth of nations. This second system actually makes debt into something valuable, negotiable and profitable, and was necessary for the development of international trade. But there is yet a third type of money, which is beyond what individuals and businesses... **the money used by nation states, which earn and spend by laws and treaties, which technically can create money out of nothing.** We will go more into this in the following pages.

To get started, let me simply observe that **the value of your money is simply what you can get for it from other people.** In some ways you can think of the value of your money being how much incentive it represents for others to part with what they have. This constitutes one of the key forms of punishment promoted by the old practices of shunning (completely ignoring the person and acting as if they were dead to the community) and exile (sending the person away with nothing to their name and acting as if they are dead). If no one can deal with you, everything you have becomes worthless! In addition, be you a person, a global corporation, or a government, when local products become pricier due to something that happened on the other side of the world, or when you have the wrong type of cash to pay for what you want, the value of money is always relative. In general, we might only care about what we can buy at our local market with the money in our pocket, but that is only true with established payment systems. This brings us to my second rule, rooted in politics, that **when dealing with people's money, it is all local.** A home in Manhattan, NYC, USA is not the same as one in downtown Moscow, Russia, even if they are physically identical...

In the following pages I will start with the local, personal exchange of money we call commerce, and cover all the way to the global government-based exchanges of value, passing through the relatively recent development of international financial and banking systems. I will also give pointers as to how to "Cash In" legally within each system.

The local level—commerce—is composed of payment systems, which range from cash and barter, to credit and debit cards and monetary instruments. Financial Services and Banking are mainly account-based means of leveraging debt and investment, feeding the commerce system with needed monetary resources. Government-based exchange is in many ways simply a service for managing power and monetary supply, based on the wealth of nations—as Adam Smith would have defined it—and promises.

You, the reader, probably noticed already that I am not into quoting important people, nor into citing other authors, save for a few circumstances in which I might think the opinion is relevant. Why? Because most economists define themselves as "macro" or "micro" or "specialized", and focus either on government wealth, or very narrow self defined areas, or on theories that they then declare universal truths—even when the facts show the opposite to be true. As I see it, the bigger picture of life indicates that all facets of human activity are important. The purpose of this text is not to highlight any theory: it aims instead to present a few observations, and propose a different way of looking at our global monetary system.

To cash in within these systems, just take the risk of being different, and continue exploring confusing ideas in reference to money, value and economics. Get comfortable and start taking notes because the ideas I will explore with you will get you thinking and wondering about your finances, the messages our governments give us, and the future. Afterwards, you might even have better ideas than I do; since I think we have a whole new field of study to look into—thanks to the surprising opportunities and contrasts offered by virtual currency, also known as Bitcoin, cryptocurrency, and others.

I. Commerce and Payments: The First Ecosystem

Barter

According to historians and experts, barter was the first form of commerce employed by human groups. This coincides with most childhood experiences of exchanging one valuable item for another among friends. So I would exchange a sandwich for a sweet, or a baseball trading card for a rubber ball, etc...

Today, in countries with economic turmoil, in which stores are often empty, the neighbor in possession of toilet paper will exchange it for milk, coffee, or bread, and many other products: barter will take place because their money is useless for obtaining these scarce resources. And there are stories of Germany after losing World War One, in which people would need a wheelbarrow full of paper bills just to pay for one loaf of bread! As I see it, this demonstrates that for commerce and payments between individuals, money is not always what you need: what you need is that each individual be in possession of something the other wants and is ready to exchange for something else. Barter has the advantage of not requiring language, and the disadvantage that you must normally be physically present in some way for the exchange to take place. Of course, you can cash in on barter by knowing more about the relative value of things than the other person.

Exchange - The Origins of Money

It is fascinating to watch children at play, especially when they have been taught that they can't just hit another child to take the toy or food they want. As they learn to communicate, we see them asking, offering to exchange something for something else, and a very simple form of barter arises. In time, they familiarize themselves with the idea of property, and the power of saying "this is mine!", and through experience they discover the relative value and relative cost of the things they like and want. Glitter and bright colors are attractive and exciting, and black, white, grey, are often less so, making glitter and bright colors more valuable to them (and to some animals). As the child matures, new measures of value arise, and many things are learned, including how to use money.

Barter, as mentioned before, is considered the most primitive form of exchange, and it is actually the ultimate democratization of value. Just imagine a virtual store in which buyers could bid with their own goods, products, and services, for those of others. This was commodity trading, with no monetary value assigned to the items being traded. According to my research, money actually came about when traders wanted something easy to carry, easy to store, nonperishable, hard to get, and defendable, that would be considered valuable in different places— therefore salt, jewels, and rare metals first started being used as currency. I will go into this in a little more detail later in the book.

So, when we study money and currency, we need to remember that the primary use of money is (and always has been) between people who want to buy and sell things within the commerce ecosystem.

Money and Commerce

As mentioned above, the main problem with barter is that it usually requires face to face negotiation and resolution. And it is also quite specific. Merchants soon found that they had trouble transporting bartered goods, and that it was often difficult to sell some of their new possessions in a timely manner. The big exception was a "three way trade route", in which the big earnings consisted of selling products back home that could only be obtained indirectly, in exchange for products or money from the first stop. Let me explain with a simple example: I want to sell records from a popular singer, and they are sold out; I find out the singer will exchange them directly (cheap) for musical equipment that a friend in another town will sell me cheap. So, I use money to buy the musical equipment, exchange the equipment for the records, and then sell the records (probably on eBay or another e-commerce venue) for the highest price I can get. This is an ideal three-way trade, and the concept was the secret of many historically great merchants who followed trade routes and knew who wanted what in each town.

Nevertheless, this could often be a cumbersome process, and merchants opted to use precious jewels and metals as a first form of currency. Local governments were usually interested in promoting trade and collecting taxes in a form that could be stored as treasure, so they started producing coins with specific content of precious metals, and a specific value. These coins were great for commerce, and easily transported by the merchants as they moved from place to place.

Some types of coin were preferred to others, and for different reasons. The important thing to remember in the payment system is that **the buyer will always want to pay the seller with what costs them less, and the seller always wants to be paid with what will result in greater wealth**. That we now mainly use dollars, euros or other national currency is just an evolution of the old coin production method: trade-based exchanges are regularly made between individuals and within organizations to **satisfy their needs, and to generate greater wealth**. Trade-based refers to non-monetary factors, including barter, that are used for defining value for that transaction, and it is similar to barter, but starts and ends with a monetary exchange, which is why it is often used for money laundering, too.

The Need for Money

Money is necessary to modern commerce and payment systems. This has been true for centuries and is exemplified by the situation the British Colonies in America experienced concerning their money.

In the 1700s, the Northeast American colonies had scarce reserves of British coin and precious metals, so no one wanted to spend their coin for local goods. They needed the "real money" to get needed imported goods. Therefore, local goods were bartered for in many ways and often resulted in unique regional markets. This story is fascinating, given American creativity and British desire for control, but it would be distracting to our purpose to go into details, so please check out the book listed in the Bibliography if you wish to read more about this.

Creating the idea of Wealth

In most historical narratives, we observe that early human communities were focused of the concentration of power, the ability to control and influence others and the environment. Individuals wanted more food and clothing, and the ability to get what they wanted. But there was a very limited supply of precious metals, jewels, or whatever else merchants wanted for their goods. Besides, these goods were themselves only available in limited quantities. There were no global markets and no means of communicating with people who had what you wanted other than physically going from one place to another, and this was very costly. Therefore, ancient communities (please note that this also applies to contemporary criminal and war faring groups that do not follow the rule of law) often resorted to raiding each other, and robbing merchants, to take what they wanted. Being a warrior, a part of the raiding party, brought the ability to acquire desirable women, bring people to work as slaves, have new clothing, metals, foods, and other property, so this gave an illusion of wealth that became very attractive for the young and ambitious, and is still seen as the "glory" element of being a warrior.

In the long run, raiding communities and robbing merchants was not productive, because these communities knew nothing of the wealth that comes from education and the development of productive economic activities. Instead, in the communities that *did* prize education and collective projects, civilization began to thrive. In time, more developed regions created armies w to defend the people from raiders and armies from other regions, and warfare became more organized. At that point, and up to the development of capitalism, wealth was still measured by the ability to collect and store precious metals, jewels, and high value property (which were called *riches* and *treasure*). But, as Adam Smith well pointed out in his earthshaking *The Wealth of Nations*, true wealth lays in a nation's capacity to generate wealth for its citizens—a complex thought if there ever was one, and one that has been **misinterpreted by those who think wealth only translates into monetary terms, and not into the standard of living and public services of the people in the nation. Of course, intangible wealth is hard to translate into numbers on a ledger sheet or a budget, but it certainly has a value.**

For the people and academics, then, wealth became synonymous with the monetary capacity to engage in ever greater levels of commerce, including the paying for human labor in the form of armies, workers, farmers, etc. Of course, that interpretation of wealth — the ability to hire others — was evidently important when kings had to raise and pay for armies to defend or expand their borders, or to conquer other peoples. After the Industrial Revolution, though, it became evident that the accumulation of monetary wealth also brought political and regional power far beyond the ability to pay for warriors, bodyguards, or weapons.

In some cases, slaves were considered part of "wealth", which followed the tradition of the warriors of old who would enslave war prisoners. Yet, this monetization of human beings, and the creation of specialized commodity markets to manage them, did not produce much real wealth, if any: keeping slaves is costly if you want them to be productive. With industrialization, it became cheaper to use women and children as low-wage unskilled laborers (until productivity gains also allowed society to stop using children). And the advent of industrial farms also made low-cost unskilled field workers expensive, due to the training needed to operate the new farming equipment. Of course, there are specialized products that still use unskilled farm hands, but at this time it seems that modern farming entrepreneurs prefer to use trained workers with specialized machines to manage higher volumes of production, and generate greater wealth that what handpicked crops produce.

The abuse of human beings, be they slaves, servants, women, children, which I personally abhor, became economically and ethically unsustainable in the industrialized nations of the late 19th Century and early 20th Century, and slavery is now prohibited in most parts of the world. The elimination of slavery has allowed technology, starting with electricity, railroads, radio and automobiles, to extend the possession of basic levels of "wealth" to all of a country's population. This extension of wealth to everyone in a country allowed individuals to be free to pursue their own economic interests, and to start the important process of innovation that has transformed Western society into one that would seem a paradise to people from the dark and middle ages. Why? Because in the 21st Century the vast majority of humans can easily satisfy their basic survival needs for food, water and shelter, and to enjoy occasional luxuries and public entertainment. As the great sociologist Abraham Maslow would point out, the motivation to satisfy physical needs is the most basic of motivations, and only when those basic needs are satisfied can we be motivated by and work towards other, higher causes.

The wealth of the nations extended to longer life expectancy, educational level, public health (often measured by the smell of cleanliness), durable clothing and tools, availability of public services, and even the rights to freedom, justice and the pursuit of happiness. During this process—and thanks to technological advances in the 19th and 20th century—the ability of national, regional and local governments to offer support services that freed individuals to work and be productive also increased. This allowed a middle class of not-poor-yet-not-rich consumers to enter into commerce and make payments at a rate that was previously unknown outside of the higher classes. In ancient societies, the wealthy (and powerful) would share these services and benefits among their family members, ensuring the continuation of their family's hold on power since they were all capable of managing their people and their wealth. Though his practice seems to continue to this day, with exclusive services and even separate educational systems for the privileged few that can afford it (as well as the selected few that are brought into these institutions to increase the size and potential of the elite community), democratic governments have also developed and offered public services, including education, that compete in excellence with those offered in private institutions. In France, for example, there is apparently only one path for higher education that leads to high government positions, pursued by both the ultra-wealthy and talented individuals of the middle and lower classes.

Wealth, as such, has moved from a focus on basic needs and possessions — the ability to pay for what we want — to a series of conditions that allow individuals within each nation to produce wealth for themselves and others, and to pursue previously unimaginable success in business and other productive activities. Electricity and other public services have brought the ability to produce and manufacture to places that were previously inadequate for highly productive activities, allowing for wealth generation wherever the decision is made to invest in needed infrastructure. This is an evolution of the concept of wealth that goes beyond the first ecosystem that is described in this chapter, and signals that there are other ecosystems that affect this one, just like a pond is fed by a river, that is fed by the creeks, that were created by rain on a mountain top. The wealthy and rich, commonly seen as possessing large amounts of money, focus instead on other aspects of wealth that will bring money to them.

Returning to the previous thoughts — how governments provide basic shared services that are elements that multiply national wealth, as well as the personal wealth and wellbeing of their people — we must now look more closely at the "middle class" or "working class" phenomenon, since it is one of the keys to multiplying the wealth of a nation, or to destroying it.

The middle class is basically made up of individuals who are working very hard to generate a better life for themselves and their families. In general, these are people who want to do more than satisfy their basic physical needs. They could be part of what some call the *working poor*, but their intent to achieve economic, personal, and social growth separates them from many of their peers, and leads to community development and wealth over time. As a group, they study and make use of every advantage available to their community to accumulate wealth of all types, not just monetary, which results in more commerce and a greater exchange of money, products and services.

In many countries, measures have been taken to protect and nurture the middle class, including labor, human rights protections and free high quality education, as well as programs to reduce poverty in general. In the USA though, the different state regulations that have reduced the ability of the middle class to thrive, including disallowing organized labor to protect employees and workers against abuses from the power of the employer, have had negative effects on general wealth of the population, which has already been documented. Basically, organized labor takes the working poor, and makes them productive middle class citizens that are highly active in the commerce/payments ecosystem, with incomes high enough to stimulate different economic activities that were previously privilege of a small minority. Of course, in some cases, local and regional governments have passed piece-meal legislations to protect workers, but the loss of freedom to negotiate — so characteristic of "right to work" legislation and other anti-worker rules — has resulted in short term gains, and long term losses in the wealth of those regions as qualified and specialized individuals move to places where they receive better conditions. It is a slow process, but it has been documented.

For the record, and in all honesty, I have worked with some organized labor leaders that fell more into the "feudal lord" model of leadership than that of enlightened humanist leaders. We humans are imperfect, and we can't measure humanity's growth and development by a few fools, be they organized labor leaders or successful business owners. Humanity's development and wealth accrual is based on how we ALL benefit and become wealthier. The few that are destructive and harmful should be taken out of the decision making process, without destroying the protections and stimulus put in place to increase our wealth. It isn't logical: but it is real.

Why? Because organized labor, organized consumers, organized merchants, and organized communities in general function to increase the wealth of their members and the rest of the ecosystem they are part of. Feudal-type concentration of riches in a few hands only serve to reduce the wealth of the nation and the population, by limiting the commerce and payment system to just a few transactions a day for the small group of participants that control cash flow.

Wealth might be seen by most individuals today as a simple monetary amount printed on a balance sheet, but in an age of electronic controls, individuals need to realize that monetary value is not the only measure of a person's or a nation's wealth. Our electronic systems have their downside because a simple typing mistake can result in an individual losing all of the wealth they have stored in a bank or financial institution, and it does not solve the timeless problem of keeping your wealth close and safe, which we will analyze in more in detail later in this document.

The Free Market that Isn't

Another unspoken truth that affects the commerce and

payments ecosystem is that **whoever has what you want, the seller or provider, usually has a clear advantage and power over you.** The normal exception is when there is variety, a number of sellers that allow you to negotiate a better deal, giving you a small advantage. Of course, in the few cases where the seller needs cash quickly, your advantage can be much greater; since you have the cash the person wants to "buy". Of course there are other exceptions, including real "must sell now" business cases, but in general we consumers are at a disadvantage because we buy to satisfy real or imagined needs, making the supposedly "free market" system an illusion. So, as mentioned before, if there are too many sellers or providers of what you want, as a customer you have a huge advantage over the seller, but lack of education and/or information on the part of consumers often results in their losing their advantage, which is where marketing and advertising come in. My experience is that, as far as price is concerned, scarcity of goods is often less important than perceived, real, or even legislated scarcity of merchants or suppliers. In the energy, diamonds, and other high value markets—including new homes—the sellers do their best to manipulate **available supply**, so that prices are kept at a specific level. Governments often also try to manipulate prices, but since the legislative procedure is very slow and tedious, quick government action usually requires acting directly through the sellers themselves, or by allowing buyers a short term economic advantage. The problem is that situations of huge advantage for sellers as well as buyers lead to reduced wealth for the community, since someone loses value in the transaction.

In the past, before the onset of global commerce,

travelling salesmen and merchants set the price and form of payment for their goods, and (as I briefly mentioned above) were the first to promote using precious metals as a means of payment and storing value, because of its durability and transportability, as well as fungibility—the ability to be freely exchanged for other goods, without losing value. For many reasons, warlords and governments picked up on this idea and started setting up their own standardized money (usually coins) for payment systems, often using a scarce metal, and also quickly set up policing groups to control the criminals that would rob and interrupt or destroy opportunities for commerce and wealth. These criminals included (and include) thieves, kidnappers, thugs, muggers, hoodlums, and also organized pirates and gangs: they all use violence to take people's wealth away from them, which raises the cost of doing business for their victims. The same applies to corrupt government officials who use the force of their authority, instead of violence, to do the exact same thing.

The Birth of International Markets

As commerce grew beyond a few merchants and their caravans, and legal protections became more reliable, our civilizations developed trade alliances, guilds, business organizations, treaties, and international commerce started to flourish, bringing greater wealth to all involved. Merchants followed "routes", and roads were built and markets established for goods and services of all kinds. Sadly, when disaster struck, or an area lost access to a trade rout, as happened frequently in places without government, commerce simply reverted back to local trade, and wealth was greatly reduced for the affected population, including the respective leaders.

Of course, this explanation is a huge simplification of world history, yet it serves to explain that international commerce requires the opportunity for merchants to not only make a profit, but also to be able to enjoy their gains in a stable, safe "home" or base. So as merchants gathered wealth and their customers acquired wealth, the respective communities and nations in which they lived also grew wealthier and usually more powerful too since they could afford armies and weapons.

In modern economies, governments pay a lot of attention to the "balance of trade" because governments understand that if their people use their money to create wealth for other countries that will result in less wealth for themselves. And there are many examples of this actually happening in the past two centuries: some countries are left with no money to pay for needed materials, much as 17th century colonies often lacked money with which to pay for tools, furniture, books, etc. from their overseas kingdoms. Interestingly enough, having valuable mineral resources is no guarantee of long term wealth for what are known as third world countries, because they must import everything else for their populations' needs. Imagine the situation of a person who owns a gold mine, but is extorted by suppliers and transporters: Human history is full of similar situations, even in recent North American history, in which control of transportation and supplies was actually used to force entire countries and regions to keep prices low, at a huge cost to the people that owned the natural resource. It is surprising to thing that "Banana Republics" and other forms of keeping nations in poverty were the result of international commerce that was controlled by small groups and specialized interests that held all the advantages in the transactions they decided to execute. Of course, history also shows this led to warfare and conspiracies, and all sorts of human bondage, and laid foundations for the Socialist and Communist movements of the Twentieth Century. As mentioned above, this situation resulted in short term benefits to a few and reduced global and national wealth as a whole. Why? Because colonies, countries, towns and regions in poverty cannot participate in the financial ecosystem and so cannot create wealth that will feed into the government and the payment ecosystems. This is similar to a predator killing off all the babies and mothers in the food chain: the males alone cannot sustain food levels for the predator.

International Commerce usually feeds the payment system, the financial system, and government treasuries wherever it occurs. Yet when mutually beneficial trade is restricted in any way, everyone loses the opportunity to make money. Thus, my experience is that most trade barriers end up punishing local commerce while enriching, for the short term, a few interests that are taking undue advantage of market restrictions in the "protected" area. On the other hand, unethical practices, including those of economic warfare, are sometimes only stopped with trade barriers, legislative protections, and strong borders. In short, International Commerce can still be a risky business even though it has become a much more common and profitable than it was just a century ago.

In the 21st Century, there is a new international commerce that actually interacts directly with the financial ecosystem: the international exchange of coin that is called remittances, where an immigrant in the US will purchase money to be delivered to family "back home". In past centuries, sending coin from one place to another was a risky venture, and Wells Fargo was one of the businesses that took gold and money from one place to another, but now these transactions are digital and make use of the banking digital systems to facilitate this form of wealth transfer.

Warfare and Economic Value

Here I must talk about the problem of wars: they disrupt commerce and they usually bring about pillage, theft and destruction. All of these activities reduce wealth —even though victorious invaders will often argue they are acquiring assets, which is only true if they are receiving a part of the war spoils/bounties/pillage/properties, which are usually abandoned and damaged buildings and goods, not the means of producing them. Wars hurt collective wealth because they simply redistribute what remains. Roman armies, for example, rewarded their victorious soldiers with farms in the conquered lands, and these lands soon became productive new colonies, thus expanding the Roman Empire. This worked well for the Empire, as long as the Roman armies were victorious for it appeared there were always new conquered lands and slaves to be distributed. But when they started losing battles, it became evident that **if you are busy attacking or defending, you cannot produce or build much of anything, and your wealth cannot grow**. Similarly, the great wealth of the colonization of America and destruction of native people's communities was twofold: the gold, silver and treasures taken by the European conquerors created a glut and depressed prices for precious metals, and at the same time great wealth was produced by creating new production facilities and products to serve Europe, including farms, plantations, mines, and fine furs. Another benefit for European wealth was the opportunity to send malcontents, criminals the poor, and other sources of civil unrest to a new land where they would progressively turn the wilderness into a source of goods for their colonial masters. Once again, this is a huge oversimplification of history, but it brings us to the topic of warfare: What the colonial powers did not realize is that the colonies were full of people who did not have ownership nor access to the wealth sent to Europe, and imports were mainly accessible only to the colonial rich – and they themselves were limited by the colonial authorities. This led to great inequities that made even plantation owners and other local leaders feel they had nothing to lose by revolting. Not all of them, of course, but war became a true means of redistributing wealth, acquiring the trappings of luxury, excitement, a sense of power, and greater money flow as the increased number of colonial troops spent their pay (in "true coin"), stimulating commerce and crime.. Hence the adage that a war will end a countries economic woes, which I really think is an illusion, since it only redistributes wealth in a very wasteful manner and kills off a great part of the productive population.

In the colonial past, recovering destroyed means of wealth production was not too difficult because most colonists had the basic skills and tools needed to go back to their normal lifestyles, even within cities. I must note that the loss of wealth that European Monarchs were facing during colonial wars become evident to them, and they "lost" the wars in such a way as to give independence to their colonies without losing the commercial ties that were still active or on temporary hold. Thus now there were new nation states that could develop their own wealth in the payments, financial and government ecosystems.

Slavery, human servitude, child labor and uneducated populations also kept, and keep, great masses of humanity outside of the wealth creating activities we have described here, but the violent and nonviolent efforts to incorporate these masses seem to correspond to when industrialization and technology offered ever greater productive opportunities that the excluded masses wanted to access. This oversimplification is relived regularly my immigrants who rebuild their lives and then request or demand representation and equal opportunities. Of course, modern travel and communications also help individuals of all economic classes to search for and find money making opportunities. But modern civilization is much more complex than that of Colonial America, and in the twentieth century, war results in destruction that takes decades to repair unless it is financed with a well-funded and supported national development plan.

This brings us to another subtle yet dangerous misperception: that war and conflict can be used to increase wealth for their people, be it in just restitution or fair distribution, etc... or that work and conflict stimulates economic activity. As I understand history, war and conflict only generates wealth for the weapons and war industry, while the rest of the populace usually faces increased taxes and costs, and shortages of many resources and products. In my humble opinion, the taking of another people's land and property only seems to benefit the takers—but as the Romans demonstrated thousands of years ago, the true increase in wealth was not due to pillage or mere redistribution of treasures and resources, but more likely a direct result of human effort, of utilizing the land and riches to generate new resources, valuables and opportunities.

Other Wealth Re-Distribution Strategies:

A simplistic example of the wealth creation potential of pillage and war would be that of the individual that inherits a small general store. If he starts using up his inventory for himself instead of continuing the commercial activity: he will soon realize that having a store can be expensive (costs and crime are constant problems) and that huge inventories can go bad over time. The other alternative is that the new owner decides to work the store, generate sales and income and maintain the existing commercial ties before someone else steps in to replace the store's place in the local economy. The income generated covers costs and can allow for the owner to increase his personal wealth directly, through commerce.

A similar experience is that of breaking up a large plot of land to distribute it among inheritors or as a program of "land reform". Without training and preparation, most individuals receiving land or don't have the skills necessary to make it productive, or to get a good price for it when they sell it for a quick profit. In my time with turning company towns into privately owned communities, I promoted social engineering programs to reduce the amount of employees who did not know what property ownership was about. The company had learned that simply giving away homes led to poverty and even community decay because the people did not feel or understand their stake in the homes. These examples might not seem to have anything to do with pillage and war, but in fact they do because they point to the importance personal effort and building productivity to achieve lasting wealth.

Civil wars are an especially painful situation, also due to the reality that power is wealth. The same issues of building wealth apply, but because the focus is on taking power and control, the loss of wealth of one side is seen as a victory for the other. Sadly, in a civil war, both sides share the same payment system and material resources that are being attacked.

In my opinion, and with few exceptions, wars of all types and armed conflict tend to make the populace poorer, and concentrate wealth among the powerful groups, who can make use of the few war-related profits that become available. Interestingly enough, there are schools of investment that focus on securing "war market" properties, goods and financial instruments, including gold and weapons, as a way to build wealth. This, once again, leads to a reduction in the number of daily small transactions that people have every day within the Commerce and Payment ecosystem, which results in a loss of community wealth. A similar situation can be seen in modern countries in which government controlled economies lead to scarcity of goods and the loss of value that is called "inflation". If people cannot find bread, they will pay huge amounts in paper bills for what little bread (or flour) can be bought. In these situations, and during warfare, barter comes into play, and even more value and wealth is lost in the process.

Wars, though, just can't eliminate the commerce and payment ecosystems, because armies too need to purchase food and supplies, and individuals continue needing things. In the past century, war-related commerce with the armies might have tended to be based more on promises to pay (by people with rifles) than on the real exchange of value in these transactions, but this is changing. Nowadays, there are exceptions associated with specific military organizations that use modern payment systems, including credit and finance, and actually make payments in real currency and bank deposits. Yet, those forms of payment tend to break down on the battlegrounds where sellers fear for their lives, and saleable goods and services can lose their value quickly. During wars there are many who enrich themselves buying and selling, but in my opinion their wealth is just a fraction of what the community has lost in the process.

Collaborative International Commerce

So let us return to peaceful commerce, which is a collaborative effort among individuals, organizations and governments. If we look at the number of transactions that take place daily, commerce seems mainly personal and local. The Payment system is mainly made up of small personal transactions, and has been this way for ages. The big change, in the last two centuries, has been that the volume of monetary transactions has grown to high levels, which include business to business and international trade, regulated by government policy and international treaties.

Using the lessons of peer to peer barter, trade, and commerce, the development of commerce with businesses, corporations and legally constituted associations—as entities able to buy, own, and pay for things and services—has resulted in the ability to transact on a much larger scale than the merchants of the past could have ever imagined. Multinational corporations often have budgets that compare with those of many countries. The great Spanish and English empires, and later the major oil and industrial empires of the early 20th Century, all generated wealth through the control of assets that generated greater ever growing budgets and disposable income. And, in the 21st Century, thanks to the development of new value and asset management tools that include artificial intelligence and mobile applications, as well as modern finance and business administration, this huge volume of business to business commerce can even take place without human intervention.

Of course, this is hard for the general public to understand: the magnitude of transactions that allow for riches to be made on what would seem insignificant details such as exchange rate and marginal cost differentials. To this we must add the new element of the financial ecosystem's quick credit approvals that allow the payment system itself to be used directly in large scale financial schemes and even large scale money laundering. This is because International Commerce is no longer as focused on sales of goods as in generating and adding value. This might seem a small difference for the financial manager, but requires a huge change for the public who does not understand this concept. Mind you, we are talking about millions of transactions a day, or more, in which the individual buyer can lose their identity and importance. Thus, it might be cheaper for a volume seller to cancel an order and refund the money than to spend time with the client on a help desk phone call. International commerce is a special part of the ecosystem.

A special note for traditional economics thinkers:

For a traditional and straightforward discussion on money, commerce and banking, I can suggest you visit the classroom webpage:

http://europeanhistory.boisestate.edu/latemiddleages/banking/, which focuses on the development of financial techniques during the middle ages, which led to today's international commercial and banking practices. I disagree with some of the assumptions the historian makes, but the ideas are sound and I will not criticize them.

I do think that traditional economics needs to focus more on the differences in the three major ecosystems I mention here, and that monetary models should be based on the characteristics described here.

II. Banking and Finance – the Second Ecosystem

Ever since international commerce (or inter-tribal commerce) I was started, risks were high, and merchants needed a way to safeguard their hard-earned money and goods; having a personal army accompany them everywhere they went was impractical, so what we now call banks came into existence: people with a safe place and defenses for money and other valuables. Banks—trusted third parties, "hawaladars", treasurers, and other names that changed according to region and language—all refer to the basic financial service of keeping other people's money safe, lending money, making payments, and vouching for international transactions and exchange. As international commerce grew, banking (and, when permitted, money-lending) became an accepted profession for trustworthy rich individuals. Often, these individuals also invested in merchants' ventures and businesses to increase their wealth as part owners, too. To refer to these first financiers, I will use the term "money bags", even though economic purists might want to classify them in other ways, since they came from diverse power structures, and in the US they sometimes came from poor backgrounds—but they all built their own treasury and ability to use their own and other's wealth in creative and constructive ways.

In time, a network of "money bags" came to be, and they trusted each other enough to facilitate new fields of commerce, and gather coin and precious metals in exchange for their services. One example was the creation of Lloyd's of London by shipping interests that could not get backers for their cargos. This form of organization benefited small merchants who up to then were unaffiliated with the powerful of their time, and stimulated commerce and international cooperation even more than the opportunity of commercial transactions did.

During the colonial age, some kingdom's monopolies worked directly with their colonies, handling all commerce within the empire and thus also handling finances, but without providing support for independent merchants and shippers. In the case of England, as mentioned before, independent British ship owners ended up cooperating and setting up contracts for sharing risks and benefits, giving birth to their own financial insurance system, now known as Lloyds of London. Here I must note that in some countries, the independent commercial sector was not allowed to develop, with the result that these countries did not develop the capital-intensive economies of today's European Union and the USA. The countries that limited their banking and financial services to those activities approved by law, or by prohibiting the services outright, not only couldn't adapt quickly to new opportunities for generating wealth, but excluded themselves from the many benefits of international commerce and increased flow of moneys within their countries, regions, and cities. My interpretation of history is that excessive government planning and government monopolies of commercial and financial systems end up limiting the growth of both the commercial and the financial ecosystems for that country, as well as that of the nation's wealth.

In general, with the international commerce that accompanied empire-building by European powers, we can observe the new commercial initiatives planting the seeds of future wealth centers, that could either store their money, make international payments, create international business opportunities or help them manage risks. At a local level, lenders might have been limited by usury restrictions, both religious and legal, but the new international merchants and financiers could use contracts, partnerships, trade organizations, corporations, and business groups as a means of making investments and **creating** local representation in other countries. These changes, including the concept of separating ownership from management, allowed the wealthy to be part of money-making ventures without having to appear as owners, limiting their risk of ridicule, criticism, and even jail. At that time, managerial and financial developments were, in many ways, similar to historical feudal organizations, and European history of the past millennia mentions many of the secret societies that were thought to manipulate governments and **regions** through their finances. Yet, these developments required the innovations of the industrial age, capitalism, and representative **government** to bring banking and other financial services into the dominant position they occupy today. In fact, it could be argued that the 15th Century Renaissance has been a key element in the birth of modern commerce and payment alternatives, as well as what we now know as the global financial system.

Three-column accounting simplified the management of cash flow and assets, and accounting also served as a bulwark for international commerce. In addition, new territories offered opportunities for growth and expansion with few concerns about competitors or local opposition. Unavoidably, criminals also kept pace with these innovations, developing new techniques for separating people from their money that mimicked the financial tools of commerce, such as Ponzi schemes and commercial fraud. However, until the 20th century most commerce was still local, between individuals who knew each other. A coercive development for international trade routes that still exists today is the blockade or embargo when governments or trade interests wanted to control a market or war broke out. Here, I must note that the art of skirting blockades and embargoes has evolved immensely, as evidenced in the drug trade and human trafficking in the twentieth and twenty-first centuries, keeping pace with the ability of international interests to skirt other types of governmental controls. I will not go into details about this, since it would take a team of experts and a few volumes to study and analyze it. Besides, this is not the subject of this book and is only referenced because criminal activities must also be considered a substantial part of commerce.

The Effect of greater International Trade

The importance of international trade cannot be ignored even if, before World War I and II, it was not given much academic importance. International trade promoted, and was also considered a byproduct of colonialism, and later of mercantilism, in which great fortunes were made and military powers were created. In hindsight, colonialism was probably inevitable because the financial backers of international trade were usually also members of the country's nobility, and saw conquest as wealth. Trading internationally in scarce resources, furs, valuables and foods pushed many undeveloped and previously unknown regions into new ways of living—some of them positive, and yet many just a repetition of feudal societies with modern amenities and armies (and poverty). But, in the late 19th and early 20th centuries, a new form of generally accessible wealth appeared, that of knowledge, and knowledge of foreign languages and culture could be used to generate income, earning, or sales. At this time, international trade also served to distribute new ideas, including those of social transformations, to the former colonies and masses of poor that had not been previously connected to the more advanced payments and commerce ecosystem, nor to the local financial ecosystem of their communities. In effect, a new "treasure", that of ideas, that had previously been considered exclusive to the higher classes of every nation, was now available to many new populations across the world. Is this a simplistic explanation? Of course! But it was foreign professionals and workers who spread the news and the message of opportunity and freedoms, acting much like missionaries, spreading their own ideas instead of religious beliefs.

This apparently new form of value, intellect and knowledge, was transmitted for different reasons, but I propose that it was a way of creating and sustaining power structures over the local population and promoting the interests of the foreign merchant who brought new knowledge to the region. The socialist and communist organizers of the early and mid-twentieth century are excellent examples of this effect In addition, the ease of transportation and communications that evolved during the ages of Industrialization and of Communication, built upon the empowerment and literacy improvements resulting from the invention of the printing press and made the transfer and multiplication of intellectual wealth easier. Here I must also note that transferring knowledge to a new population was usually a win-win situation for the merchant, who turned the good will of clients into greater sales, and when the clients increased their income they bought more from the merchant.

History shows us that rural economies that had to compete with international commerce were often at a great disadvantage: the international merchants could influence and create many unfair and destructive situations, including blockades, inciting insurrections and military intervention, to ensure they could develop a commercial or productive monopoly in those locations. The Opium Wars in China are just one notable example of the abuse of international merchants, and the banana republics of Central America were another. In addition, I will also mention the development (and power) of many multinational conglomerates and corporations with larger budgets than those of the countries or communities they were/are doing business in, which led and still leads to market distortions in those places. These distortions are not part of the Financial Ecosystem, though they may appear to be part of it: instead, such distortions arise when commercial and financial structures have the power to change and apply laws, and assume the role of government, which is another ecosystem. This point is important, because when a financial or commerce entity assumes decision making power over a population, it becomes a de-facto government, distorting the payments and the financial ecosystems and thus reducing the wealth of the region.

The expansion of Banking

With increased international trade, the rich (let me call them money bags and not capitalists) and banks started expanding their circles of influence and becoming more powerful. Storing gold and other valuables in the most secure vaults available was critical, but so was the ability to grant loans and other trade related transactions. The establishment of formal "co-respondent" relationships with banks in other cities and countries was a first step in expanding power, influence and wealth. This was followed by the creation of extensions of the bank under different names, including branches and subsidiaries, which also increased the opportunities for creating profits and wealth. These developments often preceded the establishment of laws that could control the banking activity, so abuses and fraud did occur rather regularly and the banking sector strived to demonstrate high morals, ethics and reliability of their leaders and employees so as to maintain people's trust in their ability to safeguard an individual's money. Besides, before the mid-20th century, technology didn't allow for reliable **remote** control of transactions and availability of funds, which limited the growth of banks to places within a few hours travel distance of the main offices. Telephone, radio, telex and telegraph communications did help extend a bank's ability to communicate over large distances, but local control was necessary until the last decades of the 20th Century, and the development of computer networks dedicated to the financial system. With world wars requiring nations to move huge amounts of value internationally, telecommunications were used to help systems evolve to allow international banking to become less dependent on paper documents. The invention of the telex as a secure communications system and air travel also accelerated the development of new means to control international monetary transactions within a 24 hour period. By the second half of the twentieth century, companies that formerly transported physical money and monetary instruments were developing the means to serve as money-service businesses, that could make **distant** payments and receipts, and "travelers' checks" became a common means of safely transporting wealth when travelling. Of course, these were developments that were more akin to financial instruments, credit and insurance systems, but for the public they were an extension of the banking services they were growing used to. But, until technology evolved enough for banks to share client's personal information securely and accurately, the client was kept highly dependent on their local bank office or branch to vouch for them and for the availability of their funds. Thus "private banking" became an innovation for the wealthy (individuals and organizations to facilitate international transactions and commerce. To this day we see the importance of private banking and of banks dedicated to mobilizing just a few clients' money, though global monetary and banking regulations are restricting their activities in order to curb the access of the banking and financial systems to criminal money. Of course, this is affecting the privacy that was prized in these elite banking services, but it has become evident that criminal organizations and corrupt politicians have also made use of the system.

The availability of checking accounts that could have a credit line associated with them was a major boon for long distance business and small scale international commerce. It also expanded businesses' ability to create wealth by using credit immediately, without waiting for the approval of loans—though some businesses to do not request large amount lines of credit, and their big transactions then require pre-approval of a new line of credit. The existence of lines of credit and checking accounts for small businesses allowed them to negotiate most effectively and to respond more quickly to changing needs of their commercial clients. As we see, at first it was critical that bank offices had a physical location, and transactions occurred through cash, checks, travelers' checks, letters of credit, certified checks, bank checks, or other verifiable means of transferring value that were only immediately "cashable" at the bank where the account was held (or the instrument was made out to). Traveler's checks were an innovation in the middle of the 20th Century, working within the different regional banking systems as prepaid internationally recognized certified payment orders. Users would buy fixed value traveler's checks that they could often cash in stores that worked with tourists, increasing the convenience of purchasing while away from home.

Another development that affected banks was the shift from using gold—or commodity-backed currency—to *fiat money*, the value of which was determined by law, and not by the value of the gold or commodity it was tied to. For example, up until then, every US dollar had a value in gold weight. Other money was measured in silver weight, or other valuable commodity. In truth, it is fascinating to see how creative humanity has been in determining the value of their money, but fiat currency – a concept that dated from the colonial era - was definitely a major development for the 20th Century since it was part of the advent of the Information Age. With fiat currency, banks did not have to keep huge amounts of physical currency on hand, and central banks were able to coordinate cash deliveries to satisfy demand for cash at different bank locations (branches, subsidiaries, etc.). However, this transformation was accelerated with the development of computers to collate and organize large amounts of data: once signatures have been verified, accounts and transactions could now be put up to date in a matter of hours, instead of days, and now it is almost instantaneous.

This situation lasted until the introduction of space exploration and satellites, as space-faring nations developed high speed computers and other technologies, which allowed engineers to develop systems to safely and securely share instructions between distant offices, even overseas. For example, the Telex was once such critical invention, being used for many processes as it provided secure and safe communications over physical wires that crossed continents and seas. By the 1970s, telex communications were considered as binding as faxes would later become, and encrypted email communications are now. New technologies allowed financial services to offer easily portable credit instruments, called "credit cards", which were personal lines of credit that could be independent of a banking account. In time, these evolved to include "debit cards", able to draw directly from the client's bank accounts, investment accounts, or mobile money accounts (including PayPal and other new money service businesses), once most transactions could be verified and processed in seconds.

The creation of the new financial payment systems was a boon for the development of online commerce and payment activities, allowing for the creation of even greater wealth as more and more individuals became part of both ecosystems: commerce/payment and finance/banking.

The use of Corporations for Creating wealth

This last development has been possible thanks to the expansive use of corporations and other legal entities to do business using the new technology. The Dot.com boom (and bust) of the end of the 20th century is but an example of the excitement of new small investors using technology to be a part of the stock market, the commodity market, online commerce, and other new forms of making money. These investors could often be anonymous, and they could reap profits with much fewer risks than it they had to make their transactions personally.

Many countries decided to take advantage of this new opportunity for generating foreign and local investments and became what we call "tax havens", where individuals and businesses alike could hide their monetary wealth and not pay taxes on it. This was not exactly a unique development, since the US had some states that had already offered similar services to traditional commerce organizations and financial services. So businesses started having a choice as to where their official domicile would be, and the cost of creating a corporation decreased. More importantly, in the second half of the 20th century, the use of formally incorporated non-profits, non-governmental, and philanthropic organizations set a higher standard for these organizations, and forced them in many ways to think in terms of wealth creation, too.

For example, there are international charities that started out as a purely volunteer organization, ye nowadays own hospitals and other property worldwide, and who must maintain resources on hand for any contingency that fits their mission. Sadly, some people will confuse contingency and personal wealth, and will attack their reputation of these organizations One result of these misguided critical campaigns towards non-profits, non-governmental organizations, and philanthropies, is that many now use private fundraising and financial management firms to ensure transparency, even when the costs affect their finances.

20th Century Global Financial System

In the 20th century, there has been a boom of innovation for financing commerce and payments, including new ways of raising capital and of distributing risk (beside insurance). Many stock, equities, and commodities market strategies of all kinds were evolving—including variations on fraudulent pyramid schemes—and investors loved the excitement of price and value fluctuations, where fortunes were easily made and lost.

When investors were able to work on a global level, thanks to the Internet and global communications, this development and transformation of the finance sector accelerated, thus permeating the formerly rigid and highly conservative banking system. Now, banks could charge fees for services and offer ever increasing benefits to their customers, which they gladly did. Investment strategies and corporations, including the mutual funds, derivatives and other strategies, suddenly became attractive opportunities for pension funds, local governments, nonprofits and other normally low earning pools of money because of the inflationary effect that could devalue money in a savings account. In fact, together with the advent of the global financial system, it became very common for even savings accounts to lose numerical value over time, and for the account holder to lose everything in that account, simply due to recurring fees. Thus, the "smart" holder of wealth would move money into financial alternatives that offered more return compared to their savings accounts.

As I write this I recognize my many over simplifications, yet the simplification can allow the reader to evaluate the basic ideas and reach his or her own conclusions. As I see it, the global financial system has made banking and finance very complex and full of legal distinctions that make it difficult to understand. This very complexity is why the invention of cryptocurrency is of so much interest to the technologically advanced wealth holders wherever they may be. Cryptocurrency offers the freedom to transact directly, what they call peer-to-peer with minimal or no processing fees, and also offers all the benefits of the global financial and banking system when dealing with people who also use cryptocurrency. But, the interface between the cryptocurrency alternatives and the established global financial system is still difficult to cross, though many star-up innovators are working hard to solve this issue. The Global Financial/banking Ecosystem has another answer , though: innovators are working hard at adapting the underlying encrypted technology of the distributed public ledger, that runs cryptocurrency, to handle all the existing transactions that currently run on older, expensive and faulty systems that are reliable and predictable in spite of their faults. This, or course is a developing industry, and the future will tell if the "Blockchain", as the technology that underlies cryptocurrency is called, with adapt well to the needs of the existing Global Financial/Banking ecosystem, or if it will repair existing relationships and processes in the system.

The need for Government Control

As I mentioned before, all this innovation and transformation in the fields of commerce, payments, banking, communications, money movements, and individual capacity to exchange value has opened the door to much criminal and abusive activity. Thus, legislation and regulations have been put into place, aiming to create oversight and control over systems that exchange value through accounts or third parties. Cash-based person-to-person exchanges continue to be unregulated and uncontrolled, out of respect for privacy and transparency, but in the 21st Century, the use of any service to handle money or wealth is commonly under some sort of oversight, limit, or controls.

In this sense, even straightforward purchases and sales of products deemed to be of concern for safety or health reasons are subjected to restrictions and controls based on age, residency, taxes, etc. Also, if property or commodities must cross borders, they too might be subjected to controls, due to different government policies that are officially put in place to defend the public's best interest.

Generating wealth while under strict government control is not impossible: In fact, some businesses love working in an environment where competition hardly ever threatens their profits and rules are clear cut and risks low. Nevertheless, this does have a stifling effect on innovation, experimentation and investments in start-ups. Of course, some innovators might want to follow the path of becoming illegal entrepreneurs, and there have been a few bankers that assisted these illegal businesses to get banking services. These irregularities, which were seen as a means to facilitate money laundering and financing of criminal activities, led virtually all states and nations to establish regulations over banking services, and to organize a staff of inspectors and regulators to regularly visit and inspect all banks to ensure compliance with the law. The same situation tends to arise with every new type of financial business or technology, which the respective government will regulate to prevent further abuse.

As an example, "insider trading"—the use of secret information to take advantage of people transacting in the stock market **without the information (unclear)**—is now a crime in the USA. Honestly, this could seem unfair to, for example, a company president that decides to five his family members a gift of publically held stock, since the President would only be safe from investigation if his company stock loses value! Somehow, this feels wrong, but I understand that more than one stockholder has been hurt by the manipulation of information by the company's governance structure.

Of course, this is not a problem in the case of privately owned corporations, but we need to understand that privately owned businesses usually cannot raise the huge amount of capital that the financial/banking ecosystem has available for publicly held organizations.

This ecosystem feeds from the commerce/payment transactions it facilitates, and it also feeds from the benefits of working with the Government Transaction Ecosystem. The latter exerts power and influence by means of the financial and banking transactions it generates. Government controls ensure that the Financial/Banking Ecosystem does not cause harm to the Commerce/Payment Ecosystem, and that it does not usurp the power and influence of Governments.

The creation of central banks to oversee their respective country's monetary policies has been a great innovation of the early 20th Century. In most countries, the central banks are government agencies, but not so in the USA. There, the bank-controlled Federal Reserve has a politically designated President, but the board is made up of banking sector representatives. Thus, the Federal Reserve is essentially a private concern with governmental powers, subject only to USA legislation and regulations. This design for the Federal Reserve was officially the solution to undue partisan influence on monetary policy, but there are many voices that insist that this should be changed. My own observation is that wealth has increased in the USA during the existence of the Federal Reserve, and that much of that wealth has been concentrated in a small percentage of individuals and corporations.

Storing and Exchanging Value with Stocks and Commodities

In the Twentieth Century, Stock Markets and Securities and Commodity trading became popular because technology allowed for the participation of individuals with limited means. And, with the advent of pensions and labor unions, pools of money that required investing in the financial ecosystem also generated opportunities for more wealth to be created in the financial ecosystem. Most importantly though, after gold backed currency was eliminated, many individuals and institutions started utilizing the financial system to safely store their wealth, much as we described the banking system doing with its use of vault and other storage services. Why? As I see it inflation was a main reason, and taxation was another. Trusts were invented so as to ensure wealth could be kept safe for generations, and laws protect individuals that participated in these and other institutions (including pension and savings organizations), and they grew to become a huge part of the financial ecosystem, with elements of experimentation and even huge risks for every new advance in technology.

On the criminal side, the fraud of Ponzi Schemes (also known as Pyramid Schemes) is constantly reinvented and disguised, using new investor's moneys to pay out earnings to the first investors, and doing so until a huge base of the last investors is left with nothing, because there was neither investment nor purchase of anything. This type of fraud can be very complex, when it shuffles the investments through different companies with techniques that correspond to the "Layering" stage of money laundering, and can even be extended to corporate and government organizations who believe that they are investing in real assets.

Criminals also like to use assets, stocks and securities for laundering their money, in any of the three stages of Money Laundering:

> Placement (transferring the ownership of the ill-gotten wealth in the financial system);
>
> Layering (moving the value, property, asset, money or security in different transactions meant to disguise or hide their origin);
>
> Integration (giving the ill gained assets new life as perfectly legal and well documented wealth, that is clean of all criminal traces).

As a result, at the beginning of the Twenty First Century, real estate itself has turned into an asset that is often only held for a short time before being sold, both for quick profits as well as for other purposes that have nothing to do with the original intent of owning land, housing or physical installations. Thus, the creation of money within the financial system also could be said to involve the creation and transformation of value in different assets that are used for monetary purposes.

Money Service Businesses

Sending money to other cities and asset transportation services were the origin of many banking services, but with the advent of central banks and banking regulations, these have become a separate industry that includes money transfers, check cashing, bill payments, and other services for individuals who do not have banking accounts, or who wish to send or receive money with a certain level of privacy. As the financial services used by the poor and immigrants, they are often accused of facilitating money laundering and criminal activities, yet they are regulated quite strictly in most first world countries. Phone payment systems and the prepaid card sector are also part of the money service business industry, and they have grown to compete actively with the banking system in developing countries that have huge populations with no access to modern banks. They function very well thanks to the Internet and our vast communications networks, that allow even rural farmers to use inexpensive hand held phones and computers to be identified and to participate in a financial transaction.

Some banks prefer leaving these small clients outside of their systems, so some governments are looking to these institutions as means of bringing in an ever greater number of individuals into the active (and regulated) national economy, and are even proposing doing away with cash in order to minimize the unregulated grey and black markets that still exist in their countries.

Though the financial system works mainly with digital funds, roistering the monetary wealth of organizations, countries and individuals in their computer systems and databanks, there are new forms of intangible digital value transfer and storage mechanisms called tokens, Virtual Money and Cryptocurrency that are presently being used by individuals and businesses alike, and the businesses that facilitate transactions with these new instruments or moneys are often classified as Money Service Businesses because they serve to transfer or store value. In 2017 this represents a possible transformation of the Financial ecosystem, but I have to admit that the larger financial institutions and governments are doing their best to incorporate them into their business model.

III. Government and Power Transactions – the Third Ecosystem

One of the biggest responsibilities of a government is to protect the interests of its citizens or stakeholders, if we include the governance systems for international organizations. Another is to use all means to protect the physical, social, and economic wellbeing of people within its borders. I interpret this to mean that a government has to protect its wealth and the wealth of its people, and must allow wealth to accumulate within its borders, so living conditions may improve for its people. History shows us that this requires three elements: military prowess, budget/money/treasury management, and social development (health, education, services, diplomacy, interregional commerce, regulation, etc.). The social development aspect is huge, and naturally expands as the society grows economically and technologically, as the population expects better services from its public sector. But aside from all that, one of the key areas for protecting the people is actually that of monetary supply management: basically, making sure that there is enough money available for businesses and individuals to buy and sell goods and services. This is easy in the case of an isolated community, in which barter can replace or supplement monetary transactions, but can become quite complex in jurisdictions involved in long distance and high volume commerce and exchange. In the Twenty First Century, central banks have had some difficulty in this area due to criminal interests of all types that siphon off money into the grey and black markets as well as the failure of government policies for creating wealth.

Monetary Supply in the British American Colonies

The case of England vs. its North American colonies is an interesting example of monetary supply management (or mismanagement). There was a scarcity of "real" money, since all of the British coin needed to be used to pay for imported goods, and none was left for local commerce. Therefore, the local businesses started creating new forms of currency and payment, which often led to illegalities. Local governments then issued their own "fiat" money by decree, but these new currencies presented issues as well. Many experiments took place, involving different types of local money and paper notes, until the British crown outlawed them. This lack of money for commerce was one more reason for the American people to revolt: they wanted their money, and if the British could not supply it, well they would create a government that could. This was important because the colonists had no other way to purchase what they needed from local or overseas vendors. This monetary situation was not a direct cause for revolution, but it did give meaning to the complaint of "taxation without representation".

This can be confusing, and most individuals truly don't understand money and finance outside of a few shared truisms (which are usually myths) and their own personal experience with their wealth. In a government or corporate budget, a single dollar or euro or yuan is hidden among millions, invisible in the numbers; yet for an individual, that euro or dollar or yuan or piaster might represent food on the table that evening.

Fiat and the Principle of Scarce Resources

Traditional economists frequently point out that we live on a planet with limited resources, and that among these resources just a few can be renewable or recyclable. Therefore, they base their theories on the principle of scarcity. This can be very scary for individuals, because it is coherent with our real life experience: we do live in relative scarcity, and needed goods can indeed run out. Industries and governments also worry about planning for the future, and all of them have to deal with the concept and perceived reality of scarce resources. Yet, seen from a historical point of view, humanity has managed to substitute and even find new sources of needed materials, which includes developing the ability to manufacture raw materials such as latex, petroleum/hydrocarbons, alcohols, food flavorings, textiles, and more.

As a result, what are called "scarce" resources are now only the more costly to purchase or substitute. A good example is fresh water, which has been the frequent source of conflict and warfare for all of history: the Israelis and other populations have made deserts into prosperous agricultural regions. At a high cost? Yes. but they were and still are successful at creating wealth.

Another example is gold. In this case, we should remember that gold, and other precious metals, are used not only for jewelry but also for industrial purposes. Of course, in a world of multinational corporations influencing media, "scarce" may also mean that the corporations are promoting the idea that we don't have enough of something, while they stockpile huge amounts—as is the case with the diamond industry.

Diamonds in the market are very expensive, diamonds in storage are not; wages to miners are low, wages to jewelers are high. The "added value chain" of most products (which is how much each step or link in the chain of sellers from producer to the store owner) can be surprising to outsiders. It is all relative, and for the consumer it usually does not matter, since we deal with the flow of money, not with absolute amounts. "I can afford this" is often a momentary decision based on either cash in the wallet or credit card balance, not the true price (even though we love explaining how much money we saved with the purchase). Luckily, my favorite economics professor in college told us that all the economics theories out there were unproven, and that all we really needed to understand was the "Pareto Principle", which describes—among other things—how people choose what to buy and what to do. In my professional experience, I found the Pareto Principle really applies to many economic and business problems, and I invite you to research it after you finish this book.

This brings us to the concept of "relative cost", which to the individual usually means "relative to what other people pay", or "relative to how much I've got in my pocket". Please keep the concept of "relative cost" in mind, because this is one of our major cultural stumbling blocks when evaluating choices: most of us tend to choose the most immediate or lower cost result, without considering anything else. This can be good for Wall Street brokers and such, but even the grocer knows to compare quality vs. price before making a purchase. The individual, though, often prefers the lower cost of a special sale simply because we seem to be genetically programmed to avoid loss, so not buying the cheaper product would mean we lose something. Then, at home, we quickly figure out how to cook or store the excess before it spoils. Ted Talks cover this type of behavior from different points of view, and it would seem that we need to educate ourselves to understand that huge discounts are useless if we won't use the product or don't like it.

Luckily, human ingenuity and creativity have allowed us to solve the "scarce resource" problem over and over again. Every time we have faced limitation, someone has suggested or invented a solution, and now farms produce many times more food than they used to, water can be extracted from the sea, metals and other expensive materials can be recycled, and even waste has been turned into a source of wealth, just to mention a few. From a hunter and scavenger past, we are now producing what we need through farms, plantations, factories, refineries, and even 3D printers. This has led to the apparently "crazy" conclusion that it is cheaper, easier, and better to replace something broken with a new item instead of repairing it... yet if we look beyond our immediate environment we will find that our discarded "broken" or old products are actually repaired and recycled to be marketed in poorer, less industrialized countries. This tendency has grown so much that now cities such as New York export their garbage to other states and countries, where the waste becomes wealth for someone else. Is this good? Let me just say that the principle that 'one man's garbage is another's treasure' was one of the building blocks of the oil export business, and is definitely better than dumping garbage or waste in the sea or a landfill, where it creates other problems for humanity and the biosphere.

To close this section, let me move onto the most dangerous of all scarcity theories: the concept of scarcity of value. Is Gold the measure of value? Some people think it is. Is Silver the measure of value? It has been such for many centuries, especially when the Spanish Silver Peso was the internationally recognized standard of value. Yet Spain itself found that Gold was not value in and of itself: when Spain stole the American gold and brought it to Spain, thinking they had made themselves extremely wealthy, they created a gold glut that actually reduced the value of the precious metal because there weren't enough products, goods or services to buy at the old price with so much gold available. Therefore, instead of gold being scarce, food and goods became the basis for establishing the value of gold in Spain and Europe. From "relative cost" we moved to "relative value", which Spanish financiers had not predicted. In fact, gold became an international unit of value only when governments agreed to give their national money a fixed value in gold weight, creating what we called the "gold standard", which was abandoned as twentieth century countries required a greater money supply than could be backed with their gold reserves. Our financial markets and experts still promote gold as a secure asset, together with other precious metals, jewels and diamonds.

An old joke speaks of a traveler, lost in the desert and dying of thirst, who sees before him a flamboyant restaurant and a man in front of it. He runs to the man begging for water, and the man offers to sell him a tie. The traveler angrily pushes the man away, saying "I need water", and runs to the door to the establishment, only to be told that water was plentiful and free but he could not enter without a tie.

Scarcity is not only related to existence and availability, but is also related to the relative cost it (the resource or product) has, and the relative value we give to what we want. Our thirsty traveler thought the tie was worthless to him, but the tie was a critical asset if he was to get water. It is confusing to think about sometimes, but we have all experience having to decide whether or not to accept the conditions imposed on us for a sale or walk away from what we want.

But the power of having something that another person wants really does often lead to inequities, especially when the buyer has no choice but to buy. My experience is that legislation might be passed to prohibit some unethical and even fraudulent practices, but human ingenuity as well as consumer ignorance or desperation can result in these laws being ineffective. Thus, regulation and control have become more and more necessary in the 21st Century, to avoid the nation's wealth ending up in criminal pockets.

Politics and the Principle of Fiat

At the same time that politicians and government experts speak about scarcity and market forces, they constantly apply the power of the law—or principle of fiat—to make the people (and markets) behave in certain ways. The power of law is such that it can give value or take it away, and regulations are commonly used to favor desired activities and punish undesirable ones. More importantly, young adults have not yet learned that fiat is only as good as the trust people have in it. Thus, when people decide to regularly break the law, the principle of fiat is replaced by the principle of reality.

The problem is that both the law and reality are interpreted by the people, and these interpretations are based on perspective. Therefore, a minimum wage that barely allows the poor to survive is quite different from a minimum wage that allows the poor to be active consumers of retail goods. Both alternatives have been tested in the USA, for example, and in spite of the success of using the poor and working middle class to stimulate the a national economy, first demonstrated by Henry Ford and Ford Motor Co., we still have policy makers insisting that the cost of wages hurts the wealth of the nation. Ford Motor Co. transformed the US economy by paying wages that would allow all workers to purchase a new car, which was then considered a luxury product. The multiplier effect led to higher wages in Detroit, then in all of the car manufacturing plants, and spread to the rest of the US industrial base in a matter of years, bringing great economic growth to the country. During this period of economic growth, a lot of wealth was created in different industries, and the young country leveraged its participation in two world wars to become a superpower and world leader.

The other alternative, that of survival wages, has been the norm in many developing countries, in which the low wages end up creating wealth for foreign manufacturing or commerce. It will be interesting to see how, at the dawn of the 21st Century, the USA will resolve its struggle to approve a small yet significant increase in minimum wage levels as a means of stimulating economic growth. Some states have approved a higher minimum wage, and seem to be doing better (in economic terms, and quality of life measures) _ than the low minimum wage states, but I am the first to admit that it is unwise to believe all the press releases that appear in our news media. In my humble opinion, both sides have wonderful arguments, yet they both forget that in the world of law and policy anything is possible, including legislation to regulate sunrise and sunset.

Many modern authors of "get rich" books speak about how modern finance allows the financier to create money out of nothing via the creative use of debt, but governments have the ability to approve debts for themselves one year, by decree (fiat) and then find ways to eliminate the debt without actually moving money around. Here, they use budget tricks and strategies that can be surprising to those that work in traditional finance circles, though the rules are similar. Creating money for a national government can be achieved easily through, to mention a few strategies:

- Central Bank (the Federal Reserve, in the ISA), increasing the money pool in the financial system, which goes directly to banks and other financial organizations,
- International Treaties that create debt,
- Selling Bonds and other debt instruments to generate income,
- Adjusting taxes or tariffs,
- National projects that increase cash flow,
- And we mustn't forget the age old strategy of confiscation.

These strategies don't always work, and in countries that are financially weak, the entire monetary system can lose value very quickly if the people and businesses refuse to receive or transact in that money. Of course, the principle of fiat backed by the force of a police state can keep a country using its near worthless money for many years, but it still brings the country to have little, if any, international commerce.

Besides, there are individuals and organizations in the country, including criminal interests that are experts at transforming legal decisions, regulations, and decrees into windfalls for themselves. This is often called an "unintended consequences", even though most of the decision-makers and legislators could have predicted it had they simply thought the issue through. The Principle of Fiat, as many kings and queens and dictators discovered too late, can lead to severe issues for the people, and even to greater problems for the law-makers if there is a revolt.

Of course, I am no economics expert, nor do I want to go into true/false situations about the very monetary systems that I perceive no one (or very few people) really understand as a whole. My reasoning is that government policy mainly serves and aims to keep constituents and businesses able to participate in productive transactions, sometimes with surprising results, so I will leave my brief discussion of the "principle of fiat" (the principle of law or decree) here, barely touching upon the unintended consequences that seem to be unavoidable.

This principle is truly frustrating, since populations tend to forget the mistakes they, and their government, have made, and they find scapegoats to blame for the consequences of their actions and decisions.

The Principle of Forgetfulness

When governments receive a loan, the officials already assume that they won't be in power anymore when the loan comes due. Similarly, the government that pays off a loan might allege that the money has disappeared or was stolen. In the case of what we call "First World countries", the loans are usually made through established traditional mechanisms, but in poorer countries this is not necessarily so, and the country might not have any checks and balances for handling or managing the new source of income. Special interests play into this situation by manipulating and distorting facts, and even by using outright misstatements. Thus, a popular belief in corruption arises in those countries that do not have applicable systems of checks and balances nor controls for government loans. If these systems are not put in place, public alarm might cause a cycle of accusations and prosecutions that can last years, but this does not happen often simply because the public does not care about old news, which is what I call the "principle of forgetfulness", which is also referred to as "This, too, shall pass".

Another element of the principle of fiat forgetfulness is the built-in inflation policies all governments have for their coin. With the excuse that a little inflation is good for the economy, they regularly weaken the value of their fiat currency, counting on the poor memory of the voters to hide their mistakes. Of course, when a population forgets what their coin is worth, and simply allows their government to devalue it, trust is gradually lost since no one understands what is happening, and they start considering it normal for their wealth to lose value over time. In fact, debt levels will naturally rise as people falsely assume that their debt loses value as well. Thus, the people forget that a nation's "fair wage" might have once allowed for the purchase of goods they now cannot afford. Of course this is also disguised by the cheaper prices and commodities that the global commerce system has brought to industrialized nations, which are often the result of subsistence wages in very poor countries, in an "invisible" transfer of wealth from a poor nation to the rich one.

In the 20th century, industrial and manufacturing developments brought cheaper goods and time-saving products to middle class and even poor families, increasing the wealth of industrialized nations, but this is no longer the case. This situation is truly very complex, and would seem to have nothing to do with monetary policy or our financial systems, but the truth is that money is:

- a medium of exchange when used for commerce,
- a medium of wealth creation when used in finance,
- a medium of power and control when used between governments.

Most politicians and high level managers know that control over money is power, which includes control over budgets and appropriations. The use of techniques to reduce answerability for mismanagement and corruption, especially in regions with little if any rule of law, results in their counting on the principle of forgetfulness to cover up for their activities, especially if they can create a crisis (yes, even a war) to distract their stakeholders. Oh, and for those who think that international corporations have are not part of government, I will agree that they cannot be part of the United Nations, nor do they have the prerogatives of traditional countries, but they have been participating in this government ecosystem for a very long time.

Other politicians rely on the principle of forgetfulness to convince followers that their country or community is in very bad shape, when it is actually doing fine. They shift the focus on the same small difficulties of previous generations that have been ignored by established government entities, and promote these difficulties as symptoms of a greater ill, destroying trust in the economy and thus reducing the power of the government. Informed citizens know that this is false, but a good share of the public has forgotten their past (and their gains), so they go along with the complaint. In extreme cases, this has led to uprisings that have destroyed beautiful cities and even entire countries, or have broken economic engines that were built over generations. Right or wrong, the politics of pulling down what exists is common in human history and I would say it is surprising that our civilization has survived in spite of it.

Historically, college students are prime candidates for messages of "change", even when false, mainly because they really like looking for new ways of solving old problems, and they have a tendency to focus on problems and quick solutions without looking for the lessons of previous generations. Many idealistic students and individuals supported communist, socialist, populist, anarchist, etc., proposals worldwide, and history points out their later disillusionment with the results of their achievements. Why? Because when they took up the revolutionary ideals, they lacked the data and information to analyze and evaluate what they were being told and promised. We should also note that history includes many governments that have restricted the growth of wealth among their people through corrupt and unethical practices, and the idealistic students and educated youth are usually quick to pick up on these inequities and act against the squanderers of their people's wealth. For this reason, a good educational policy is required to maintain the wealth of a country: people need to be educated to understand where their own wealth, and also their nation's wealth, is actually coming from.

Government Transactions with Constituents

Thanks to the many changes 20th Century technology has made possible, modern national and regional governments have the capacity to interact directly with constituents, without having to go through local representatives who traditionally served as power brokers, both in democracies and in autocracies.

One government agency that has historically interacted regularly with individuals and legal entities is its tax collection unit for the respective government. This unit receives information and answers questions directly, without having to go through an intermediary or political representative. This was true in the historical past where farmers paid with whatever they had, and the tax collector had soldiers backing him, to modern times where everything can be done by computer. Of course, in some cases the banking/financial institutions will be used for collecting information and forms, and validating the identity of the taxpayer, but even then there are places where taxpayers can interact directly with their government.

The importance of the direct transaction between the taxpayer and the tax agency lies clearly in the fact that this is one key presence of the government within the Commerce/Payment Ecosystem, and any distortion in these transactions can have large impacts on the trust taxpayers feel towards their government representatives. It is also the way the government enforces the use of its currency, paying employees with its money and collecting taxes with its money, too.

Another area subject to government-constituent exchanges of value is that of keeping people safe, mainly in the policing aspect, but also in the military aspect. The policing aspects are mainly for control of crime and keeping the peace, while the military aspects are normally focused on external threats to the physical integrity of the nation, yet now it also needs to cover other types of threats. These interactions may have a notable monetary component, especially with the budgetary processes and payments to people and organizations, and they are meant to ensure all aspects of the individual's wellbeing and wealth.

Some governments also offer healthcare services, retirement insurance plans, emergency assistance, etc. directly, but these services are often highly criticized for their "bureaucratic" nature when people have to make use of them, as due to the huge volume of recipients or clients, they are rarely able to offer personalized, flexible services.

When these government services replace private industry, they have two competing effects on the wealth of the nation:

- first, the effect of reducing direct costs for the individual that receives a free or subsidized service, which allows for greater individual wealth creation,
- second, the interference in the possibility of wealth to be created by private ventures that offer the same service.

Which one is predominant? I really don't know, because there are many elements to consider. As for the health practitioner, in the case of Canada and other countries that offer public healthcare services, I've read most health professionals are government employees. But, to be fair, I've observed that in the USA private health system, many health professionals are becoming employees of hospitals and other health service providers due to the high insurance, litigation, and administrative costs that accompany a private practice.

Considering other areas in which governments can offer services, my observations indicate that these services are often a source of contention between competing political parties, and that there are always those who say that it isn't cost-effective, that government does a poor job, and other arguments. Different arguments often focus on budgetary issues, or on equality, justice and opportunity. But not many individuals look beyond short term results, and power struggles tend to be the priority as the decisions are made.

One recent example of this is that of the US Postal Service, which has faced budget restrictions, and was competing with private package delivery services. In 2015, it faced major restrictions, but a change in the services offered by the private delivery services actually resulted in new business opportunities for the government backed service in 2016. The private parcel delivery services are still doing business, but the postal service has taken back part of the market.

In the case of education, we often see public education co-existing with private religious schools, and private independent schools. They all must meet similar basic criteria for each grade level, since there is almost universal government supervision of all education organizations. Yet, the private schools are usually reserved for those that can pay their fees. If the public schools have high quality education, private schools will also offer top quality education with better supplies and installations. But if the public schools are undesirable, I've also observed that some private schools may also offer poor value for their fees due to the lack of competition.

With respect to police and military, in some countries there are private police and militia services that complement the government, but once again these serve only those that can pay, creating wealth for their owners but not serving the public at large—which is probably in need of their services, too. Whether or not these services help increase the wealth of the nation is a good question, but they certainly are used for guarding the treasures and property of the very rich and powerful.

To conclude this section, then, we should always consider whether or not and how wealth is generated or enhanced by having the government supply specific services and products. In the cases of shared resources, history points to the benefits of government control and distribution. In the case of critical services, where human lives may be at stake, government must at least maintain close control over quality and safety. And, where the survival of the nation or country is at stake, then it would seem that government should be completely responsible for it, with public oversight.

IV. Wealth Accrual and Control

In this section of the book we will evaluate, in plain English and without a lot of financial terms or formulas a few different methods of gathering, accruing, and also controlling wealth. We will look at how the different functions are trying to gather information from all three ecosystems, but without understanding the characteristics and needs of each. And, by not understanding the needs of each ecosystem they can affect the total, global wealth of the nation. For some individuals, individual wealth accrual is the greatest priority and for others the priority is that of creating social capital instead. The question is: what is the best store of wealth, of value, for a nation as a whole? Individual capital or social capital? Each community and nation must decide for itself, of course.

Wealth Accrual

Wealth accrual is applicable to individuals, businesses, corporations (and other legal associations of individuals), and governments. People measure their wealth in terms of the value of their property, assets, bank accounts, investments, etc., all of which can be given a monetary value. In a later chapter we will look at whether or not this is a good strategy. For the sake of simplicity, I will point out that wealth is, in monetary terms, "the value of everything you have minus the value of everything you owe".

Therefore, at the payment level we can easily conclude that the more we have, the more wealth we are gathering.

If we own a home, with no mortgage, the value of the home is ours. If we own a car, paid in full, it is ours to keep, give away, throw away, donate, etc. Property is owned, and the owner is totally responsible for caring for it and maintaining it, or not. Interestingly enough, property is so linked to the individual who owns it that, if the property causes harm in some way, a court may rule that the owner is responsible for repairing the damage.

Money, if in physical form that you hold in your hand, counts as property. Thus, some people like lighting cigarettes or cigars with paper bills, and others make souvenirs in machines that will roll-stamp messages on coins. Coins have metallic value, sometimes even more than the "face value" of the coin, but Paper Money is actually nothing but a monetary instrument, similar to a check and it represents a specific value for the financial and banking system, and is usually worthless if the government backing it up is overthrown or conquered. So, what is it that we own when we have money? We own the value of the metals or paper that it is made of, and we own the socially agreed upon value of that coin or bill.

If your money is in a bank or financial account, instead, or in monetary instruments or stocks, then all you own is an "I owe you" from that particular institution. And, if your money is held in a government account, then it is technically more of a promise to pay—though you can use that promise as a form of payment for future taxes or other government debts, subject to some rules and regulations that should be checked out before you may the payment. The USA's habit of sending out "tax-return" checks for amounts paid in excess during the previous year is surprising to people from other countries in which the government rarely pays its debts. But it certainly serves to make people not only pay taxes in advance, but to file their tax forms early in order to get their excess tax payments back.

So, to conclude this section, let me simply say that individuals and legal entities accumulate wealth in the form of property and other assets, and they often measure their wealth by use of a "Balance Sheet" which combines their assets and their liabilities to determine how much wealth is truly available if everything were turned into cash. This, of course, is wonderful for government controls and taxation, which is beyond the **scope** of this book.

Wealth Control

At the financial system level, the rules are different from the payment system: since debt generates more money, the key concept here is control: control of information and of monetary reserves. This helps the government level calculate the nation's wealth, which is a combination of the wealth of the people (payment system, now controlled by the financial system) and the banking and finance industry, combined with the budget and international promises that may exist. The importance of the payment system is evident: If the payment system falters for any reason, the financial system is stressed by the request for loans that have higher risks, and the consumers that conclude that they don't have enough money end up not trusting the system or their money.

This situation can also be caused by money laundering and

the influx of a proportionally large amount of money that is the product of criminal (and thus uncontrolled) activities. Price distortions, value bubbles and other elements can create a host of problems for the financial system, since legal interests rarely compare with the amounts that a criminal will pay to make illegal funds seem legal. So the government ecosystem in a number of countries has gradually increased its capacity to use the financial system to control and tax all forms of wealth moving through the financial system, which has created opportunities for tax havens and regions with few or no controls over corporate entities to receive ever greater amounts of cash to insert into the global financial system. One organization, the international Financial Action Task Force has been gradually forcing different countries and jurisdictions to change their laws and eliminate banking and ownership secrecy, including corruption and tax evasion as targeted crimes.

But these efforts mainly affect the population that cannot pay lawyers and accountants to control their personal or corporate wealth. Those individuals and organizations can control many aspects of their wealth, having the means to own and protect valuable assets, as well as in productive activities that not only produce a profit, but serve to extend their power over their surroundings. Unless the ultra-rich want to transfer their wealth from one coin to another, or move it from one place to another: in those cases, they find themselves having to prove that their funds are not criminal, which can get to be expensive in time and fees. The alternative modern technology has offered, and which is being tested as a means of storing value safely is cryptocurrency, which was designed to be exempt from financial system controls and limitations.

This will be expanded upon later in this book.

Effects of Concentrating Wealth

Another concern is the accumulation of so much wealth (or control over wealth) in such a way is that the different ecosystems can be manipulated, and the flow of money that generates wealth is throttled and even choked by just a few individuals or interests. In the Commerce/Payment system, financial monopolies have a similar effect in that the products or services the consumer wishes to purchase are all in the hands of a single seller, with the difference that these individuals hold most of the money that could go into the ecosystem.

The paradox here is that the monetary and financial reserves of big business can limit the ability and freedom of other businesses to compete fairly for customers. This inequity, which limits the flow of money in the economy by reducing salaries and prices, serves to limit the amount of innovation and opportunities for wealth creation for everyone in that population. In this sense, the greatest incentive to the economic motor of the USA in the early twentieth century was not the war economy, which had shortages and rationing, but the incorporation of women into the workforce, earning good wages, with labor unions ensuring that workers did not slip back into poverty. Another example is that of the big railroad monopolies had lower operating costs, but were unable to deal with competition from truckers and airlines, which offered flexibility and opportunity for new businesses. It would seem that, for the railroad industry to once again generate wealth, it would have to do what 21st Century entrepreneurs call "pivot", and change to create new income streams that generate more monetary flow in and around their assets and services, instead of being public services that generate power in the government ecosystem. A good model to think about is that of a modern shopping center that promotes sales in a diverse group of small shops and big convenience stores, gathering and serving their regional community in symbiotic relationships that benefit everyone, including the shopping center managers. The existence of the three ecosystems within these examples might seem confusing and paradoxical, but it works, and it generates wealth of different types.

Adding Value To Wealth: Government protections

With the advent of international trade, local merchants would normally use "coin" and precious metals, but individuals and businesses also used script, tradable notes, personal credit, commodity exchanges, and other value exchange systems. It took a long history of stable government and societal structure to establish enough trust in "fiat money", which was backed up only by a government promise. The evolution of value exchange mechanisms was necessary because of the volume of value being exchanged daily in different communities, and the need for a way to control these exchanges of value and wealth.

For all of these solutions for paying for goods, there were cheats (and thieves) that would make people lose their wealth and demand government protections, so governments started insuring:

- that all coins had the right amount of metal in them,
- that a police existed to control the criminal element,
- those government-made coins were available.

But in time, after the 15th Century Renaissance, with the economic transformation of Europe, commerce often lacked government coins for doing business normally. So, banks and big merchants, as well as local governments, started creating their own money, which led to all sorts of additional problems, until modern governments took over **making and controlling (overseeing?)** money production, including means to detect and capture counterfeiters. They thus became trusted authorities to ensure the value of money. With these changes, the concept of fiat currency (money created by law) took hold, and was tried out, in different places of the world.

In general, the first experiments with fiat currency ended as failures, since the temptation to abuse the system by simply printing more money was irresistible to politicians, and they ended up making the money worthless. Once the financial system was able to share the risk among all merchants in an area, though individuals might not trust fiat money, commerce continued using it as long as it still had some value since the merchants found no better substitute for coin than this.

Monetary Deposits

The idea of deposits, of having someone else take care of your money, was also probably a result of early commerce: people would put their money in the hands of a local supplier, so they could make purchases without having to carry cash or valuables. They could also prepay for future purchases, and soldiers or travelers could ensure that their families had food and supplies while they were away. Established merchants were trusted to keep their word and not steal the money, because commerce was a long term relationship, and trust was generated over time. In this sense, new salesmen or merchants were not really trusted. At this time, branding was personal and leadership was critical for commercial success.

Once specialized services started growing around money and payments, the idea of a banker or financier also became common. Banks had reserves of money that could be invested, and thus earn profit for both the banker and the depositors. One solution to the issue that arose quickly was that of cooperation: shippers wanted to have ways to reduce risk of loss - of money and goods - and money did not need to be physically moved if the bankers at both ends trusted each other and kept their accounts well. Of course, surpluses could exist, but these were probably put to work quickly before a local chieftain or king decided to levy new taxes—which they often did.

Back when kings and governments used precious metals to mint (make) coins and certify the value of their money, the country's treasury reflected its wealth. But, when the movement and concentration of capital became responsibility of a financial sector separated from the government, this created a new power struggle — one that continues to this day as the government is obliged to protect the system that holds the country's wealth while taxing productive activity as much as possible in order to maintain its army, police and other services that make it powerful.

Secured Investment

Another concept that arose from commerce was that of "secured investment", in which investing in a business venture usually made you a recognized part owner of the venture, as a way to ensure payments and returns. Nowadays, in the 21st century, secured investments involve contracts and legal assurances that did not exist in the far past, but the idea is that risk is greatly reduced with a secured investment. Now, for those of us who have lived through severe monetary devaluations and financial/economic disasters, we understand that with fiat currency your "secured investment" is only as secure as the stability of your economy and government. Therefore, as the ancient romans used to say, "Let the buyer beware". This is still good advice.

Here I must also mention the issue of modern fraud that I mentioned before, that many fraudsters use the concept of a secured investment to get individuals to give them their money. The individual believes the fraudster, and even convinces friends and family to also give money to the fraudster because they are "investing in a sure thing".

In truth, the individual must verify each and every proposal that is made to them before handing money over. And always, yes always, ensure that they get a written or printed receipt for their money.

Creating Wealth and Value

In this section of the chapter, we will take a brief look at the different mechanisms that are used for creating wealth and value in the 21st Century, within the 3 ecosystems. These examples are only a few of the many money making strategies available to individuals, and most of them are now being automated by financial technology innovators.

Payment Systems

In the 20th Century, a number of technological advances improved how individuals and financial businesses handled money. Aside from the advent of computers and digitalization of records, the financial industry was growing in leaps and bounds, and the stock markets were very active in financing wealth creation. At first, individuals started relying on checks, and companies like Western Union and MoneyGram got busy sending money all over the world, as well as handing payments, which banks also did. Afterwards, it became possible for people to pay via electronic means. First, credit cards were used as a payment system, and soon debit cards came on the scene to help people who did not want to incur debt.

The different payment systems available to consumers now allow for users to receive detailed reports of their transactions, and make it easier both to make transactions as well as to manage wealth.

Debt

Debt has been an interesting issue throughout history. Since debt involves risk, there are multiple religious injunctions against it. The risk is always greatest for the debtor, since the debtor as very few choices. Yet, debt has been constant throughout human history, probably starting when communal property was replaced by individual ownership and possessions. This became much more complex when laws started regulating how debt could be documented, and a lender had the power to enforce the payment of the debt, and nowadays it is a specialized area of business and law.

For the financial and banking ecosystem, making loans is a way of creating wealth. And for very smart merchants, taking a loan to finance a business transaction can also generate great wealth, if the transaction is a wise one. Thus, we hear of "flipping houses', dealing in precious metals and jewels, stock investment strategies, and other ways of using other people's money to create more wealth for the merchant, but we rarely hear of the individuals and corporations that lost all their money. Interestingly, there are individuals who lose money regularly, but are still seen as successful simply because when they succeed, they make remarkable profits.

In addition, there are financial services that insure debt, so that the financial institution can limit its losses. Thus, a bank will have insurance against losses in its mortgage portfolio, consumer credit transactions, etc., and these costs are simply transferred to the bank's clients. Therefore, in dealing with debt, the Financial and Banking System will always make money, even when it seems they will not—with two big exceptions that result in a loss of wealth, as we will see later in this text: mismanagement and criminal activity.

Deferred Payments

Many societies have a custom of helping out a new business with a "gift" of a substantial amount of money, with the understanding that once the business is prosperous, a similar "gift" will be given to another new business. This effectively creates a non-interest bearing loan, as well as a network of connected businesses that support each other, and promote their shared interests.

Some governments criticize these financial mechanisms, because they may be used for money laundering and other irregularities, yet this is only due to lack of data for transaction analysis and tracking. Personally, I would think that the wealth that is created by these mechanisms should be sufficient to pay for the necessary data collection and interaction.

Legally binding promises to Pay

Often called "financial instruments", of which checks are but one example, most civil codes recognize the value of a note declaring that a debt exists, together with the terms of payment. Called "IOU" (I owe you), payment letters, etc., they are simple yet legally binding documented promises of payment. In the US, the figure of a verbal contract also exists, where witnesses can attest to the existence of a verbal obligation to pay a specific amount.

Credit

Though a creation of the financial markets, the line of credit has a long history in the payment system, in which merchants would offer goods that would be paid for in the future. Historically, it was more common for individuals to pre-pay for their family's expenses when they would be away from home, but merchants would then easily extend minor credit to the family since they trusted the individual to pay them back. Of course, there were occasional misunderstandings, illegalities and problems with this system, so the banking system created a more impersonal alternative: a line of credit for the person's accounts at the bank.

In the 20th Century, with the advent of modern accounting and computer systems, lines of credit were made much more flexible, and nowadays all individuals in the banking system have access to credit of various types. These different lines of credit create more money for the bank to lend, as explained before. This expansion and availability of consumer debt, and the associated income it generates, have made FinTech, financial technology, a huge industry that is creating innovative strategies for personal account-based money services that include financing into their products. Besides, FinTech is transforming the way payments for goods and services are made into a very simple process for seller and buyer alike. This shift in how individuals see their money and their wealth is still evolving, because most consumers are now conscious of the huge debt trap that consumer credit represents for them. In addition, fraud and theft seem to be becoming more common in the banking and financial services, as the computer systems that handle these transactions are being regularly subjected to cyber-attacks to steal information and change records.

Stock Market

Stock Markets are another complex financial system that would require tomes of writing and great expertise to explain. Basically, it started with the concept of offering property—called equity—in different corporation's ownership structures—called stocks. But this quickly extended to include different types of financial instruments and securities, able to generate capital for investment and investors. This accumulation of capital and exchange of values has become a major wealth generator for many local, regional, and national governments.

In developing countries, having an active stock market is a measure of pride, even though they often show high volatility, having few stocks, and being subject to government interventions and policy changes, as well as manipulative behavior from buyers and sellers. Wealth can be created and lost in these volatile markets, because with high risk comes high gains, or so the stock market experts say.

Commodities Markets

I am using this term to describe the different specialized exchanges (formal and informal) of products and services for other forms of value, which promote trade and commerce, generating wealth and new business opportunities for all. Some of these markets are simple commerce/payment ecosystem activities, but others are much more complex and involve financial and banking activities and technologies. Much individual wealth can be created and lost in the high volume commodities markets, for they combine elements of the two first ecosystems: Payments and Commerce, and Financial.

In all honesty, I do not want to enter into details about the commodities markets because in the USA and Europe they are highly regulated and any suggestion I make could become controversial.

Consumer Financial Services

A new development during the 20th Century was the formal establishment of businesses that helped the unbanked and small consumer have access to financial and monetary services.

In the US they are commonly regulated as "Money Service Businesses", and they are a critical element in the international and regional legal movement of money and credit among workers, migrants and families. New financial technologies that make use of cell phones, hand-held computers, etc., called FinTech, are revolutionizing this market, and are regarded as competitors with the banking system for these categories of consumers. The movement of money and its associated fees within the payment system generate wealth for all involved.

Global Foreign Exchange

With the advent of fiat money and computer technology, there has been a rise in popularity of the business of making money via invisible foreign exchange mechanisms that allow simultaneous buy/sell transactions in separate markets with different exchange rates (called "currency arbitrage"). One effect of this is that financial analysts now often refer to a miniscule variation in an exchange rate as a "huge loss" or "huge gain", which is only true for huge transactions. For the small consumer or merchant, exchange rates have a great impact on the price of goods and services, and can affect the trust people have in their own currency, leading to changes in the perception of the wealth they hold. Once common and interesting observation is that of tourist travelling to countries where their money is worth much more: thanks to the exchange rate, those tourists feel and are seen as very wealthy. The opposite is also true, so travelers from countries with an unfavorable exchange rate feel that everything is extremely expensive wherever they go.

Many countries, including the members of the European Union, have attempted to even out the effects of foreign exchange rates by sharing the currency of a strong economic system—with mixed results, especially when a specific country does not generate sufficient wealth to pay for its needs.

Collateral – High Quality Assets

As a final note to these few areas I have commented, is that of collateral. Within the payment system, an old form of lending was institutionalized: what in the US we call pawn brokers. The concept is simple and was developed as part of the payment and commerce ecosystem: you leave an object of value (the collateral) to guarantee payment of a loan, and if you do not pay back the loan plus interest (or fee), the object will become the property of the lender. Within the payment system level, the lender meets the borrower and it is the lender who decides whether or not the collateral or guarantee is a high quality asset sufficient for processing the loan. But this is usually not the case when we deal with the financial system: the financial system can often assume the risk of fraud and overvaluation of collateral because the loan itself becomes an asset for the institution that lends the money. This has created huge problems for central banks, when individual financial organizations lend more money out than they have available, or promote other irregularities that drain the wealth of the financial system, generate unnecessary risk, and reduce trust among clients and investors.

The paradox is that high quality assets used as collateral are often limited in their wealth generation potential during the time they are used as collateral. For example, a housing complex that produces rental income is a wonderful asset as long as the rental income is higher than the maintenance costs for the building.

To protect the financial system, most central banks promote low levels of inflation that lower the value of the debt over time, though financial fees and interests tend to maintain, or even increase the value of the loan vs. the collateral—which can lead to a perception of loss of wealth on the part of the borrower. The big exception, of course, is that of borrowers who leverage temporary valuation of an asset against the new investments made with the borrowed money. They thus transfer the great investment risk to the lender, in exchange for an asset that over time is not worth as much as the original valuation said it was worth.

Is Money still a Measure of Wealth?

Some might be horrified by this question, but it is important to think about it. Robert Kiyosaki and his Rich Dad concluded that money is not important: assets that produce income are. Wealth in the form of money is taxed, subject to fees and loses value with inflation. Money in a bank account can actually run out without the owner doing a thing, and—even worse—banks will close what they call "inactive accounts" if the owner is not making periodic withdrawals or deposits.

Money might be the way banks, financial advisors and the government measure wealth, but in the 21st Century that is the equivalent of measuring your wealth by what you have in your pockets: easy to lose, though it is also easy to keep track of.

In the three ecosystems there are predators that feed off of other people's wealth. This is a characteristic of all ecosystems: predators consume the weak and dying members of the system, and communities develop strategies and means for protecting themselves from the predators. Call it natural selection at work, but it is still a real risk for those who participate in all three ecosystems. Money is very attractive to predators, so communities have identified other forms of wealth that can produce money but are not as easily taken away by predators.

At this moment I can hear thoughts of "buy gold!", "buy stocks!", "land is the answer!", "get a government job", etc. and I believe that, while being true, all of them are also wrong. Why? Let's take a look at these four examples of common wealth accumulation advice:

- Gold has been a valuable asset for millennia, and it is just as attractive to predators as money is. I am speaking of real gold, not gold-backed anything which you cannot store in a vault and get back

whenever you want without it having changed. Technology could soon leave gold as valuable as iron, though, once it is no longer a scarce commodity.
- Stocks and equity investments in corporations and businesses can be excellent long term wealth depositories, but they require study and long term strategic thinking to be truly reliable as wealth. And in the case of publicly owned corporations, short term minded management could leave the long term investment worthless.
- Land is one of the most traditional investments and depositories of wealth that an individual, family, or business may have, but it can be difficult to sell in a hurry and can occasionally have high maintenance costs, therefore it is sometimes seen as a liability. Real Estate is a perfect example of how the development of the Finance/Banking and Government Transactions Ecosystems has made this asset (real estate) less attractive as a means for storing wealth: they both facilitate taxation of the asset and both usually follow the rule of "use it, or lose it". Mind you, the old rule that "possession is 9/10 of the law" still holds, but now you must not only possess the land, but you must make it produce more than it costs to maintain it. Interestingly enough, there are still places in the world where you can buy land and just hold on to it on paper since no one is interested in it, but population growth is slowly changing the definition of abandoned property and squatter's rights.
- A job with the government, or with any traditional and apparently secure organization that offered 1960s style Japanese "birth to death" benefits, has

proven to be a myth. The airline industry was the first to discover that the two new ecosystems let the owners acquire even more wealth when they let their companies go into bankruptcy and—in the best of cases—transferred the unfunded or underfunded pension plans to the US government. In other countries, instead, the employees who had trusted the promise of future benefits were left with little or nothing. Private industry now often utilizes this strategy, creating wealth by taking worker's contractual benefits away, and this has resulted in a rise in populist and socialist sentiment—which assumes that the government won't take away the money entrusted to it for the future protection of its people. My experience with the USA's and Venezuela's government managed social security insurance programs is that politicians try to do the same thing that private industry has done, and only an informed and educated populace can control these irregularities.

So, what are we to do? How can wealth be secured? As Robert Kiyosaki suggests that his Rich Dad would say: invest in assets that produce more income, so your income can come from more than one source. Just as the wealth of a nation should be measured through its industrial productive capacity alone, the aggregate or sum of all of the wealth of its people and legal entities also needs to be measured and factored in. A family that relies on one person's job alone might have wealth in the eyes of others, but its wealth will always depend on that one family member's job. In the past, workers were supposed to have loyalty to their employer, and though it is still a desired trait it is one that must be cultivated and based on mutual trust, not on the threat of unemployment. Financial advisors always tell their clients to "diversify" so as to minimize the risk of losing wealth when one investment or income source fails. As a result, we see the knowledgeable investors picking and choosing carefully, and distributing their wealth into what is called a diversified portfolio, consisting of real estate, stocks, bonds, precious metals, and other investments. In this sense, author and economist Richard Maybury has some fascinating thoughts and suggestions, though his interpretation of the global economic system makes him predict that everything will soon come crashing down... and his logic is impeccable if you assume that we live in a world of scarcity.

Network Marketing is a modern development that is generating much wealth in the Commerce/Payment Ecosystem. In network marketing, there is an emphasis on person to person commerce (though modern technology is key to their success), and the different styles of marketing emphasize that credit and finance drain the wealth of the developing business. Step by step and sale by sale, the network marketer learns how to produce income, reinvest in the business, and grow it until enough wealth is being produced to invest in property and other desired products and services.

In the Finance/Banking ecosystem, the modern stock market—exemplified by New York's Wall Street—is also a fascinating study in wealth creation and accumulation within the ecosystem, and also quite confusing since there are new developments every day as financial innovators learn to use developing technologies to find new ways to create wealth. If we consider financial services to be wealth production vehicles, then our Wall Street type executives are probably comparable to car dealers—but they serve in the Financial/Banking Ecosystem, which offers much greater volume of earnings.

In the Government Transaction Ecosystem, it is difficult to measure how wealth is being accrued, mainly because true data on these transactions and the transfer of power are usually vital secrets for national security. In this sense, our government leaders are constantly looking at the other governments they transact with, and try to find the best return on investment, which is usually not monetary. This is why it is so easy to criticize government policy: results cannot be seen in the short term, except in really surprising and usually tragic cases. For example, when the USA convinced the rest of the world to use the US dollar as global currency, it also made the dollar a target of all money laundering and criminal financing schemes. There is a fascinating TED Talk about how this event actually allowed for multinational criminal and terrorist organizations to rise and thrive, since they were no longer tied to the local currencies of wherever they were active.

This issue, and the fear that fiat currency would lose all value—as Maybury has been predicting for years—led a group of computer programmers to discuss the issue, and in 2009 one of them—under the pseudonym of Satoshi Nakamoto—proposed a new monetary unit and electronic means of controlling it. In this vision—which included the new technology being used for contracts, governance, storage, as well as commerce—the Financial/Banking ecosystem could be replaced by technology; although, personally, I believe that human beings will always want to deal with other humans for some of the services offered in that Ecosystem. This invention was called Bitcoin, a form of cryptocurrency, and the software technology that ensured its functionality, a public yet secure distributed ledger, was declared "open-source" so anyone could share it and improve on the idea. As hinted to above, cryptocurrency participates and can even replace elements of each of the three ecosystems, and to this date, wealth stored in the original cryptocurrency wallets is private and secure. Nevertheless, cryptocurrency is of limited use when we consider the huge volume of transactions and value that are present in each of the three ecosystems. It holds promise, but needs to mature before the innovations can make an impact—good or bad—on the ecosystems.

Regional and Global Wealth Creation

My interpretation of Adam Smith's "Wealth of Nations" is that the wealth of a nation is the aggregate wealth of all of its stakeholders. For example, in a Kingdom, the Treasury is the main depository of the wealth of that nation. In a democracy, though, this is more complex because the "Treasure" that finances the government and the country's needs depends on a yearly budget that is adjusted by predictable taxes (democracies avoid confiscation, in spite of what libertarians might allege) and planned expenses. In democracies, and other mother governments, they also use the Gross Domestic Product (GDP) as a measure of "wealth". Yet, as the USA and other countries have already demonstrated, the invention of 20th Century Fiat Currency and the global financial system allow for some countries to go far beyond the established budgets, and even go into serious debt of different types with no apparent short term consequences. How can this be?

The first key to understand "how" is that just as the financial system of fiat currency is fueled by credit and debt, the international inter-governmental monetary exchanges are controlled by a specialized "central banking system", which is fueled by promises and strategic interests. These international inter-governmental monetary exchanges are also coordinated by the World Bank and the International Monetary Fund. In this manner, the Greek government of 2016—clearly in arrears in its government obligations, and with its currency in tatters—was able to handle the financial pressures of the Syrian refugee crisis (or migration, if you will), also with the support of the European Union, who feared this member state could succumb to the humanitarian disaster.

Other countries that are technically "broke", or even in default because they refuse to pay old debts, also continue functioning for decades, simply because—in practice—a country cannot go broke, even if its population is living miserably and no other country wants to lend them anything. Commerce goes on, and governments continue negotiating and regulating.

In these cases, where is then the profit in supporting these broken economies? The profit actually lies in keeping the money flowing. As I see it, there is political gain (non-monetary), and the profit in maintenance or creation of markets for broken economies, where the aid of a "helpful" country can only be spent on goods and services from that very country: giving wealth that will come back very quickly to the donor. Besides, multi-national corporations can find ways of making money working with these broken economies, gaining advantages and properties in the short and long term that they otherwise would not have received.

Another example of this governmental economic level is that of the International Monetary Fund's "Special Drawing Rights", which give the country (that must have a strong economy) the right to expand its money supply internally and to third countries, subject to few restrictions. Becoming a member of this Club is considered the financial equivalent to being a permanent member of the UN Security Council. Yet, this allowance is useless if other countries, central banks, investors, speculators and such are not interested in your money or consider it worthless. In that case, the country's government could simply make do with what it has, sell international or national assets, or maybe even deal with some sort of parallel or dark financial service that will extend credit to it. This, of course, includes granting undisclosed political or special services to other governments or organizations. And for those who would criticize these governments, all I can say is that a government's prime directive is for the country to survive.

Fiat means "by decree", and fiat currency is given a value by law. In open economies, the market itself can change the value of a given currency relative to others or to commodities, but central banks officially keep an eye on these valuations in order to protect the wealth and economy of the nation. Yet the ability to control the wealth and economy of a nation is not yet a manageable science, because most economists confuse the three monetary systems and combine them with other financial and commodity exchange mechanisms. Therefore, there are investors (often called speculators) who purchase different fiat currencies that they think will be growing in comparative value, and they use many means to influence other financial and monetary players, including governments and the public, to make decisions that will result in a profit for them.

For example, a country with a declining value in national stocks, and inflation in food and basic commodities prices, usually has a currency that is falling in value. Please note that in this example I will not consider corruption or other types of crime. The central bank and government become worried when their money is losing value, and they devote much effort into trying to control inflation and failing markets. These governments will even be glad when speculators purchase its coin, since otherwise the government itself would have to buy its money on international markets (using foreign exchange that it has hopefully accumulated as "reserves" for buying imports). Meanwhile, financial and commercial interests in the country are strategizing how to make money from this situation, or at least to avoid losing money. The traditional investors then often start buying the money, playing a game in which fractions of a cent (figuratively) on each coin can turn into hundreds of thousands of dollar (or more) equivalents, due to volume. Social media gets into the game, and creating a price bubble that has many effects. While that price bubble exists, though, the central bank and government develop and pass policies to correct their economic and market weaknesses, and bring real value to their coin. This is mainly contained in what I have described as the financial monetary system and trickles down into the payment system. Other foreign governments, though, are generally in favor of avoiding the economic collapse of any fiat currency, so they will use their fiat coin to buy up the failing coin and ensure that the price bubble does not burst for the country that is in trouble.

Continuing with this brief example, let me note that in some cases—like that of the USA vs. China in the early 21st Century—the value-rich country will invest heavily in the other country's debt, properties and businesses, which help it insure a captive market for its products. Of course, fiat currency being a truly new monetary innovation now that technology allows true control and validation, it is still hard for governments to ensure that their currency's value will remain stable, and that the country's wealth will continue to grow.

V. Integrating the Three Ecosystems

As far as I know, no-one is looking at how to integrate the three monetary systems. Instead, we observe a lot of hype and salesmanship aiming to manipulate markets and businesses into creating opportunities for investors to make money within the financial system. Government and Central Bank specialists also tend to be focused on the financial markets, and rarely look at the human ecosystems that involve payments, finance, governments, and non-monetary activity. This has become more evident with the introduction of virtual currencies to the unbanked sectors of Africa, which have brought millions of new actors into regional and national markets—as well as promoting cryptocurrency use among the general public.

The issue is, as many economists have pointed out since the creation of fiat money, that it is really easy for governments to create money and for special interests to take advantage of the government on one side, and the general public on the other. Depending on the writer's morals, people who take advantage of ways to get money for nothing (or for lies/falsehoods) are called thieves, frauds, or even reformists (or another nonsensical term). But, truth be told, there is much diversion of funds into individual accounts, and these can create problems for a country and community when the funds are siphoned away from where they were intended to go. Aside from the criminal aspect we briefly discussed above, the bigger problem is that resources that were meant to help increase the wellbeing and wealth of the citizens. Sometimes, the siphoning off is perfectly legal and authorized, and is simply the result of people taking advantage of a loop-hole, error, or even some of the rules of that ecosystem, but the damage it causes is the same as that of a predator that decides to eat only the females of its prey and thus reduces its future food supply.

Each individual is taught the rules of at least one of these ecosystems, and they know how to benefit from specific conditions in them. Thus a good salesman could be said to have mastered the rules of the Payment and commerce ecosystem, and a professional investor or financier could also be thought to have mastered the intricacies of the financial ecosystem. The same is for the governance and power ecosystem, which allows individuals to monetize their influence and power in surprising ways – surprising for those that don't understand the ecosystem, of course. These rules and intricacies will be analyzed separately from this text, and will probably garner the attention of many economists, sociologists and authors once the concept of the ecosystems is accepted. I, myself, can't wait to see what will be proposed for each of these ecosystems.

Why speak of Ecosystems?

An ecosystem defines the pattern of relationships between different organisms that share a location or a process, and that can be studied as a unit because different parts or organisms are linked to each other, and need each other to survive.

Our Payment and Commerce ecosystem has buyers, sellers, merchants, consumers, products, property, money, and payment technology. These elements have the same pattern of behavior worldwide, and marketers take advantage of this when promoting specific products and services. On another level, this ecosystem is composed of human beings: what they have, what they want, and a medium of exchange. In the respective chapter, I tried to describe this pattern of relationships without going into too much detail, because ecosystems can become very complex when looked into in detail.

Once the Payment and Commerce ecosystem grew, it required the creation of a new ecosystem to support it, and the banking/financial ecosystem evolved out of key sellers, buyers, consumers and suppliers. Also, with the invention of money, governments and wealthy individuals became the providers or suppliers of money and of other financial services. These governments and wealthy individuals actually seems as service providers to the public at large, though the relationship was actually different from that of a contractor: Governments held the power of life and death over their subjects, but they also had the national treasury, which made them key players in establishing the supply of money for their country, and wealthy individuals could influence government representatives.

Once the banking and financial ecosystem grew to a size in which global transactions were possible, money supply control became more difficult, so the Government Transaction Ecosystem evolved and is still evolving. In this system, individual commercial transactions are almost invisible and seemingly unimportant. This is because the participants in this ecosystem are basically government leaders, Finance Ministers, and other gatekeepers for monetary policies, legislators, central banks, and the news media, though every country will have a slightly different group participating in this new ecosystem.

However, all ecosystems develop self-regulating feedback loops to protect themselves against one organism destroying everything. Thus, economists can speak freely of the free market process, by means of which if sellers raise their prices too high, fewer people will buy and they will find an alternative for the expensive product or service. Within the commerce/payment ecosystem itself, the principles of scarcity, free market, and forgetfulness might actually seem to be reliable and true, but I suggest that it is only true because of the desire of the ecosystem itself to survive and grow over time.

Homeostasis, a form of biological inertia, means that human systems tend to be stable and unchangeable until the participants do what humans do best: they change the rules and transform their environment. The 20th Century transformation of banking and financial services, and the creation of a global system for controlling transactions, has been an example of this tendency. The creation of fiat currency, combined with central bank and government transactions to manipulate currency value and controls, was yet another transformation. These two changes occurred almost simultaneously, because each depends on the other for its existence. As a consequence, the Commerce/Payment ecosystem also evolved into a global network of local ecosystems, all tightly connected to the other two ecosystems on a global and local level.

As in any ecosystem, we will find parasites, symbiotic organisms, hunters, and gatherers, and many other parallels to a biological ecosystem, but this level of detail will probably be developed at a later date, since it does require careful analysis, data collection, and comparison studies. But the reader can think, and reach some preliminary conclusions based on personal experience with the different levels.

Money Laundering and Corruption

Now we will look at the criminal element that regularly acts contrary to the purpose of creating wealth for the nation, preferring to take it for themselves through illegal and unethical means. Money Laundering is similar to corruption in that it diverts moneys intended for multiplying the nation's wealth into other, often distant, pockets. By taking away the wealth of individuals that actively participate in economic development, criminals reduce the wealth of the country, and can even distort public budgets and services. For poorer countries, money laundering often is a drain on needed foreign reserves— though the financial system usually has no direct objection to moving the funds around, since they do not benefit from increasing the nation's wealth.

The payment system level is pretty transparent, though anonymous payments in cash or other means for illegal products and services automatically bring with them the risk and problems associated with money laundering. Still, at the payment level it is feasible to track the money via transaction analysis, because transactions are tracked by the government and banks. At the financial level, in turn, funds aggregation, investments and interest payments, as well as commodity and money instruments, among others, make things more complex, though record keeping is much more detailed. Here, fraud and money laundering can be covered up, hidden, in different ways, since financial and banking laws are not the same in every country, and smart fraudsters try to work, when possible, where their activities are within the law, or where law enforcement is lax. To counteract this situation, there are laws that hold all persons, natural and corporate, to worldwide responsibilities—but this kind of legislation is still being tested in the courts due to their extraterritorial nature. Lastly, the Government and Central bank layer itself is so complex that it is easier to prosecute individuals for corruption and bribery than to detect corporate and multinational strategies to abuse the system.

Therefore, We can briefly conclude that payments often require financing, and finances often require government backing and controls, while government just requires the votes and public support to allow its voters to feel that wealth is growing in the nation. This last layer is not quantifiable, which is why it is so hard to understand: all is based on trust, perception, and perspective.

Criminal Wealth

As a side note, criminal money also has its corresponding three ecosystems, which run parallel to the open, legal ecosystems, though they have slightly different rules, as they do not follow the rule of law, and are instead based on the principle of *might makes right*. In this sense, they follow the pattern of feudal warlords, who accumulated wealth and established their jurisdictions.

In this dark economy, the payments ecosystem mainly

runs on cash transactions, and different forms of barter or service exchanges. In some locations, the legal financial system's services can be integrated into the criminal activity, but it is accompanied by the risk of being targeted by the police. The criminal financial ecosystem is primarily based on power brokers who are also financiers, and use cash, prepaid credit cards and other anonymous monetary instruments to distribute money and collect payments. However, in what is called *money laundering*, a good part—if not most—of the payments to the criminal finance ecosystem are brought back into the legal and regulated fiat currency financial and banking ecosystem, for use in legal and lasting investments and activities. The transitory nature of property within the criminal ecosystems makes it extremely desirable to put money and possessions into the traditional, legal, fiat banking, financial and registered property system. And criminal organizations will actively search out those jurisdictions with legal protections that hide true ownership, to ensure that their laundered wealth cannot be easily stolen or confiscated. Though it is fascinating to study, since it is very closely related to the issue of trust in the global economy, money laundering and the financing of criminal and terrorist activities are topics that will have to be explored elsewhere.

The third, government transaction ecosystem has its hidden parallel in the transaction arrangements between criminal organizations. These also reach agreements, make promises, and exercise power. They mainly use cash for payments and commerce because of its anonymity, but do not need to control the supply of money because they siphon off currency from the legal, regulated, fiat currency system itself. To siphon money from their nation's wealth is simple, because their law-breaking clients pay in cash, and when they use other financial services to pay, these services can help launder all of the illegal proceeds. Thus, the Central Bank function of ensuring a stable flow of money within its country actually feeds their corresponding "dirty finance/banking" and "dirty commerce/payments" ecosystems. Money laundering experts cite the amount of dirty money siphoned off to be from 10% to 15% of the global transaction volume, though officials in some countries insist that they have much lower levels of dirty money flowing in their country. I encourage the readers to decide for themselves, though I admit I can't understand where or how that 10% was determined. Whether or not it is true, FinCEN (the US's Financial Crimes Enforcement Network) has certainly detected and documented huge volumes of criminal money being illegally put into US banks and money service businesses.

The Unbanked and Cryptocurrency

Though they are two different subjects, the onset of cryptocurrency—a non-fiat form of money that exists via the Internet brought the possibility of individual control over not only personal and corporate transactions in the Payment system, but also over financial and banking transactions. However, the technology and businesses to facilitate advanced financial transactions with cryptocurrency are still being developed. This possibility—an individual having their own banking facilities in a cell phone or computer—offered an opportunity for inclusion of poor and previously unbanked populations. Companies such as M-Pesa quickly took advantage of it, and made its parent company, Vodafone, a major financial player in

Kenya and other countries.

Mobile phones are certainly becoming hand-held links to the global economy and markets, even hand-held bank systems, in many ways, and the banking/financial ecosystem has embraced these changes. It welcomes FinTech innovators that decide to work with VISA, MasterCard, PayPal, Amazon, and many other huge international "payment systems" tied to an account-based financial service. In this sense, the traditional "wallet" is now being complemented by software that creates electronically managed accounts, and allows individuals and organizations to make and receive payments with an electronic device, as well as offering the possibility of accessing other services available in the financial ecosystem, such as credit, insurance, money transfers, currency exchange, check deposits, point-of-sale, and more.

With Cryptocurrency, there is a promise of having cheaper and more transparent transactions, but as of 2017 the promise is still a promise: cryptocurrency is not yet user-friendly, nor can it handle transactions with the ease and speed of traditional credit card electronic systems. Banks and other financial players are experimenting with their own digital currencies, but have had limited success, except for mobile payment systems, such as M-Pesa, which are handled within a cellular phone carrier's customer account system.

Of course, part of the difficulty is that government transactions are not taking place with cryptocurrency (which is not illogical considering cryptocurrency's present price fluctuations), nor can cryptocurrency handle even 10% of the volume of government and central bank transactions—much less 10% of the daily volume of transactions within the global financial and banking systems (their electronic controls, communication and ledger systems). And, of course, we mustn't forget that the financial support functions of insurance, accounting, budgeting and wealth management, still need to understand cryptocurrency and the Blockchain, finding it easier to continue using the approved and well known traditional technology.

But in some ways this is a great advantage of cryptocurrency, from the point of view of individuals and organizations with high volumes of money that they do not want tracked by the governments of the world: Cryptocurrency can be a huge store of value for them, **as long as they all agree to use it and keep its value at the pre-established level.** This agreement among the ultra-rich individuals and organizations would be similar to shared contracts in which cryptocurrency would be recognized as the preferred means of storing and transferring large volumes of money in a transparent yet very private manner. The transparency and privacy aspects of true cryptocurrency would help this group minimize their risks of loss or confiscation, while ensuring long term security of the asset. This would be similar to the present day agreements as to the value of diamonds, pharmaceuticals, art, etc.

These agreements to maintain asset prices at specific levels have already been documented (and sometimes even prosecuted as price-fixing) though sometimes the free market concept is used to allow for price variations, bubbles and even crashes to be used to increase wealth and disguise the manipulation. Is this manipulation real? Maybe not, maybe it is simply the product of imaginative journalist's suspicions, but it does not matter until government representatives decide to investigate and act upon the suspicions.

This value that cryptocurrency offers is one that governments in general do not like, since it is very difficult to regulate, and the ultra-rich have greater capacity to establish independent power systems within the third monetary ecosystem of government. Apparently criminal organizations have already attempted to achieve this, but their focus on short term gains and the ease with which they break the tacit value agreements have encumbered their efforts. And, as I often mention in my role as Co-Chair of the Cryptocurrency Standards Association, the transparency of the Blockchain distributed ledger makes it very, very difficult to hide your activities and identity when the international police agencies are investigating. The elite do not really mind police oversight, because it serves their purposes of safety and security, which is yet another plus for utilizing cryptocurrency as a medium and long term solution for wealth accrual and storage.

VI. Cash In

After learning about the different forms of wealth that each of us can access, and the basic or general 3 monetary ecosystems that I have described, I certainly hope you have started thinking about how you can literally "cash in" to the different opportunities that we usually don't even notice or have been taught to ignore. You can cash in within the Payments and Commerce ecosystem by selling what you have, both physical and intangible (knowledge, mastery, skills, creativity, etc.). You can cash in within the Banking and Financial ecosystem by utilizing other people's money or property, investing your own to create new money and services, or by using financial instruments and strategies as products and services to be sold in the Payments and Commerce Ecosystem. And, the prize of them all is when you cash in on the Government (Governance) and Power ecosystem, where you have others providing you with money, property and services. We will go into this in more detail a little bit later.

Each ecosystem has its rules, and please note that each community can have variations of these rules according to their traditions and culture. And when we observe what seems to be irrational behavior on the part of buyers, investors or even governments, we should remember that there could be an unidentified desire, addiction or even passion (love, hate, lust, fear, attachment, greed, anger, etc.) behind this behavior. And, lest I forget, when you decide to cash in, you must be wary of camouflaged predators or other risks to your wealth.

One example I have experienced is the cost of migrating to a new country: when you move you often end up spending or investing unwisely, much like the new home or car buyer often ignores what is a good deal or option. For that reason, many multinational corporations make arrangements to supply their expatriates with housing and services until they learn to handle themselves in the new environment and culture. I worked at this and observed that when you are in a new culture you lack information, and must rely on behavior patterns you learned as a child from your parents, which can be outdated or even misplaced. After being overseas for decades, when I returned to my hometown as an adult with a family, my old home seemed cramped and what I thought were ample savings "disappeared" very quickly. Besides spending in "vacation mode", I rejected good investment opportunities, listened to bad advice from well-intentioned friends and family and luckily focused on creating wealth in the long term, not short. I had learned overseas that a single arbitrary government decision could wipe out savings, investments and more from one day to another, and my apparently illogical bias against some proposals was based on the idea of not stealing or using hype to promote myself or my businesses. This earned me a lot of trust, and the trust of others is a form of wealth, especially in the Governance and Power Ecosystem. It took me well over a year to learn the rules for New York City, and I paid for my mistakes, but I was naturally invited to join other community leaders and their organizations, and in a few years I naturally gathered political influence and was elected to different mainstream party positions. It involved a lot of volunteering, but as we will see later, it also gave me many opportunities to benefit.

Newcomers to a community sometimes run the risk of lawsuits and huge errors by not knowing the local ordinances and laws that correspond to their new homes, especially when interacting with someone who does know the rules and wants to take advantage of the newcomer. Been there, suffered that, as a young adult and lately, as a mature parent. And I really hate it when people say it is part of the learning curve… But newcomers also have a great advantage, when they are willing to work for it: they see missed opportunities and ways to make money that the locals might not recognize.

So, how **do** you cash in? Well, I will assume you learned the basics of every ecosystem already. And I have to warn you that I am neither "expert" nor economist that can eliminate your risk, because profits are always accompanied by risks, large or small. But, as someone who wants to present a new way of moving forward with your money and your wealth during the 21st Century

Renaissance, I will propose a few alternatives I'm sure you will find useful.

Payments and Commerce Ecosystem:

The first rule for cashing in in the Payments and Commerce Ecosystem is to be aware of costs and income. Think of everything's real value, and sell what gives you the most earnings.

The second rule, to save for the future, does not work well if inflation is higher than the interest your bank and financial instruments pay. And, if you are saving in gold or other valuables, make sure the resale price covers inflation. But that does not eliminate the value of saving for the future: even if your savings in money or valuables have lost value, you are like the squirrel in a hard winter that might have lost half of his hoard, but still has enough food buried in the ground to survive until spring. In this sense, wealth is having what you need, and saving is a way of building wealth. Hoarders, for example, seem to believe in saving as much as possible of everything they like so as to allay their fears of poverty. Some extreme cases hoard money obsessively, living in scarcity and working as long as they can while accumulating assets they do not or will not enjoy. And yes, the newspapers have a field day reporting on these cases when they appear. But, if that very same hoarder suddenly decides to cash in on the things in storage, holding garage sales or –better yet - using eBay or another online selling service, many of the assets you or I might consider worthless could end up creating tangible wealth that the individual can enjoy.

The third rule I always consider is that everything is relative. *One man's garbage is another person's wealth.* Being conscious of the relative cost and benefit of every transaction we make gives us an opportunity to identify how to cash in on the transaction, especially if we deal with relative benefits or costs in the other two ecosystems that are part of the commercial or payment transaction. One common relative cost/benefit is a government job: Usually low paying but with wonderful benefits. Hidden costs are present, but so are the hidden opportunities for creating or gathering wealth. For example, and surprising to me, I've met people who don't want government jobs because they would have to disclose their finances and would be limited in some of their economic activities (this sometimes happens to government appointees who suddenly discover that they have "conflicts of interests"). So within the Payments and Commerce ecosystem, buying and selling assets, products, services, even garbage, has relative costs and benefits that give many people an opportunity to cash in for what they want.

The fourth rule, one that is regularly applied in commerce, is "buy low and sell high". And this applies to many forms of wealth.

> For example, when should you buy the basic knowledge you will need to hold a job or build a business? As the illiterate farmer who moves to a city can tell you, learning basic skills as an adult is very expensive both in time as in low salaries. The best time to "buy" this basic knowledge and skill set is when we are children and young adults, and our brains are biologically primed to learn everything we are presented with. Another window of opportunity to learn new skills and acquire knowledge is during illness, vacations or retirement, after the children are grown. It costs nothing in time and you avoid boredom. Many colleges offer free courses for seniors and adults, and the new knowledge or skill can be used to develop new income streams. One interesting opportunity here is that of adults who help children with homework or building other skills, where they can learn from the children about new technology, opportunities, and changes in their community and culture.

Another example of "buying low and selling high", described by Robert Kiyosaki, is using money you do not need to buy assets that will produce income for you until you find the time to sell them at a good profit.

This section is very brief as to how to cash in within the Payments and Commerce ecosystem, mainly because most of us have already learned the basic rules and can even search for "how to make money" books in the library as we figure out how to follow through with our decision to move in a specific direction.

The Banking and Finance Ecosystem

Cashing in on Banking and Finance is considered an art form by many because most of us don't understand the ins and outs of what we might consider "wheeling and dealing" and using other people's money. Worse yet, many individuals think that banks and financial institutions take unfair advantage of their clients, and will point out the inevitable fraudulent individuals to prove their case.

At this point, I have to point out that record keeping and information are key elements for cashing in within this ecosystem because banking is dependent on the "three ledger" and more advanced systems of accounting and record keeping, as well as legal norms. But to understand your financial strategies, you might need a computer specialist and mathematician's explanation to make sense of the data. In its infancy, banking involved using the cash from deposits to give out loans and use the interest from the loans to pay their expenses and small earnings to account holders and bank owners. This was mainly due to the fact that all records were hand written, and balance sheets were audited, reviewed and approved individually, by hand. Nowadays the use of computers and high speed communications allow many forms of making money legally and illegally within this system.

So, the first rule I propose for cashing in is that in the banking and financial system all value is measured in money. So, if you find a low money value but high income stream value asset, this could be an opportunity to buy, and if you have a high monetary value asset that you don't like or that you know has little real value to you, you can sell it. One example is related to foreign exchange, in which a business asked for a bank loan in a third world country and immediately purchased dollars with it. A few weeks later, the government officially took over the bank and froze bank accounts for a period of time while they decided what to do. Of course there was a crisis in the country, and many feared for the amounts in their bank accounts, so the financial whiz at the business convinced the owners to start offering to buy frozen accounts at a huge markdown, often paying cents on the dollar. If you are wondering why they would do this, it is because months later when they had to pay back their loan, they told the bank that they were paying with the funds in all the accounts they had purchased. Needless to say, they made millions – of dollars – legally which were promptly reinvested in the business. Though governments have "capital flight" when their entrepreneurs and businesses don't trust the local economy and currency, this is often an opportunity for some to cash in. Of course, if you do not have money in the banking and financial system, you can't look at value differentials.

The second rule is that if you don't understand what you are doing, and don't trust the person advising you in the matter, the risk of loss is really high. Though in finance and banking "too good to be true" can occur, it is always based on some sort of knowledge and opportunity that some people use to make a profit. When you trust someone honest who knows what they are doing, you are usually safe. Yes, there is always a risk, and you should know as much as you can about the risks and benefits of your transaction, but trust in your banker or financial advisor is critical, too. As mentioned before, if you simply want to store value for a time, then almost any conservative investment or deposit will serve, especially if your moneys are guaranteed or insured by the government. Oh yes, do you trust your government? Some of my extreme isolationist friends, who believe in living off grid and off public records, prefer investing in gold and other assets that are hard for the government to control, and they accept the risk of theft and squatters and prepare themselves to deal with it. Of course, they have very limited activity within the banking and financial ecosystem, and it is by choice.

This leads us to the third rule, which is that you can't cash in if you are not part of the system. The unbanked of the world cannot earn interest, invest in bonds or other financial instruments, and ask for commercial loans, etc. simply because they have no credit or monetary history within the system. I know a family who worked with cash only until they decided to travel overseas. They were quite wealthy but had never needed a credit card and they realized that modern tourism was less expensive and less risky if you used a credit card. But, they asked me, how can we build a credit history and get a high credit rating that will cover our family trip? My advice was simple: first buy everything with credit and pay it promptly. Simultaneously they were to get one or more credit cards, with low credit amounts, and max them out, and pay the full amount at the end of the month. After two months of this, if the bank hadn't offered to raise their credit, they would ask for an increase in the line of credit which they did a number of times. By the time their trip came up, they had credit galore, a great reputation in the banks, and had not spent money unnecessarily. They now also could cash in on low cost commercial lines of credit thanks to their new reputation as good, reliable clients.

The fourth rule is simply that greater risk offers greater returns in this system, and vice-versa.

In the 21st Century, the Banking and Financial Ecosystem have offered services that substantially reduce risk in Payment and Commercial transactions. Most of us feel that it is worth paying for the safety and peace of mind these banking and financial services offer, and we recognize that said safety and peace of mind serve as a form of wealth. They are valuable to us, and it is in this overlap of the two systems that many people cash in on this monetary ecosystem: they use credit and payment terms, and other strategies to buy low and sell high, and to reduce costs of the products and services they sell. In general, and for most of us, the big financial transactions that can give us opportunities to cash in are beyond our monetary capacity, unless we use other forms of wealth that can be used within the system.

The Government (Governance) and Power Monetary Ecosystem

*"**Power** tends to corrupt and absolute power corrupts absolutely."*

(19th Century Historian Lord Acton)

As I have mentioned, governments and large organizations have budgets, procedures, and a pattern of revenue and expenses that are normally used to control what they can and cannot do. Control is important because of the huge potential impact of the decisions and actions of this ecosystem on everyone within it, and because history is full of examples of the truth of Lord Acton's words. Corruption and fraud are the eternal temptation to those that hold power, and it is possible to do it without technically breaking any laws (because laws can be written to allow certain actions).

As I wrote these paragraphs in my first draft, I saw that most of my words were warning and that I had to be careful not to write instructions guides on how to abuse this ecosystem, mainly because it is a system that few people really understand and are able to work with. As an example, I will point out that the term "Machiavellian" is used more as a criticism than as a term of respect. The same is said of social engineering. The image I see is of a

Machiavellian individual or social engineer setting hooks with bait that uneducated people bite and get caught with... 'Evil fishermen abuse the public trust' will probably be the headline of the media reports!

Sadly, if you lack information on your culture and communities, you are at a huge disadvantage in the government and power ecosystem, where image, leadership, forcefulness and presence are often more important than trust itself. As the old adage goes, "The Queen doesn't need to be a lady, but must always be seen as a Lady". Similarly, a government leader must be respected (often feared) by his/her peers. Of course, as we see in many countries, military or brute force can also serve to take control over this ecosystem, but in these few paragraphs I will exclude the use of physical force because it is often illegal, unethical, and/or abusive.

One excellent example and caricature of some of the benefits available in the government and power ecosystem is "The Chairman's Wife", describing the spouse of a very powerful individual who has no power of her own, yet inspires respect and fear wherever she goes, dressing, speaking and acting as a person with full authority. As an example, working as an airline manager I was sent to the airport where I did not have security clearance. I had my secretary send in the application, knowing it would take days to process, and put on a three piece suit, power tie, and leather briefcase to go to the airport in the scorching heat. Looking forceful and decided, I passed security many times without being stopped, and used the "Chairman's Spouse" technique to enter all areas that required my presence. The other airline managers were shocked at my luck and laughed at my "overdressing". It is obvious they had not read Dale Carnegie's classic book **"How to Win Friends and Influence People"**.

Similarly, when I knew I faced a difficult situation (in a bank or court, or bureaucracy) I would do the same, and would go directly to the top decision maker, with positive results. Please note I did not and do not abuse this characteristic, because if the true authority perceives any sort of manipulation or falsehood the consequences can be grave. But it is possible to "cash in" to the benefits legally, if you can resist the temptation to abuse the system

In public administration I was taught about the experience in a very honest northern European country of a team of import license processors who would usually emit all the licenses on a specific day of the month, following a work system that was fair and kept the work flow balanced. One day the supervisor received a visit from a gentleman who asked that his permit be expedited (given quickly) and without offering a bribe he simply said he would really appreciate the favor. The supervisor, knowing all the permits would go out soon, said nothing but told the gentleman that the permit would be coming out promptly.

A few days later the permits went out normally, and then, the supervisor received an envelope in the mail with cash. Please note that no laws had been broken, nor did the work team dispense any special treatment. But the word went out among the commercial sector and the work team started getting many "gifts" and came under the attention of their internal security and police forces. In spite of their complying with all laws and not requesting anything, it was determined that they were receiving money improperly for the jobs they received a state salary for. This is why many large organizations have a "no gifts above x amount" policy, and Great Britain passed a very strict Anti-Bribery Act. Besides, these policies and laws considered gifted services and goods are considered to have an equivalent monetary value.

The "two adult rule", for example, is used by teachers, caretakers, doctors, etc. when they want to ensure transparency in treating with minors or individuals who could be seen as being vulnerable, to be able to prove that there was no abuse of power or influence. This technique, as well as body cameras, recording phone calls, etc., is a protection against abuse for all parties involved, though the apparently vulnerable individual might not understand it. Briefly put, it allows for documentation that may ensure transparency in all transactions. In this sense, secrecy can serve to hide and even promote abuse, though it can also be a key tool for leaders in this ecosystem.

CASH IN!

Within this ecosystem, value lies in many of the activities and influence of individuals with some sort of power, and it is possible to gain wealth there, without breaking laws or gaining notoriety. Knowledge and information are key tools for achieving this skill. Having said this, we can move on to how individuals cash in legally.

Here I will once again point out that theft and fraud are not ways of "cashing in". Even within a kleptocracy, where illegal activities are common, individuals are often made an example of when someone powerful wants to punish them. Even if the illegal activity may be considered a side benefit of the ecosystem in those communities (free pastries for the Police, for example) this reduces the community's wealth and so cannot be considered a benefit. But authorized giveaways or permissions are fair game. In all cases, abuse of all types, including involuntary servitude, are at the very least unethical and definitely hurt the community's and nation's wealth.

Ethically acceptable benefits are mainly the explicit benefits of doing a job well, which includes prestige, participation in events, authorized gifts, trips and materials, even and speaker's fees once out of office. In fact, there are benefits that the individual might ignore simply because he or she did not read the employee's manual. Basically, as long as it is part of your job and is not a special advantage unshared by all your coworkers, you can enjoy it and even use the experience for future income streams once you are out of the governance position. The military, for example, offers the opportunity to receive specialized training that is often critical for a non-military career path. And the "GI Bill", as it is commonly called, offers free college education to veterans. Of course, when some individuals don't know how to use the different benefits they receive from this ecosystem, they might complain that it is unfair, but just as information is critical in financial transactions, the same can be said for governance and power transactions.

Rule number one, then, for the government and power ecosystem is probably to "be in the know", which is to have all the information available before you need it and plan accordingly.

Cash in on your governance and power opportunities by understanding that if you are giving a service, you can enjoy the benefits that are allowed by law. In some countries, members of nobility can receive all sorts of monetary and in-kind benefits, and they learn about them as they grow up from their families. Corporate executives do the same when they mentor junior executives on the "perks" of the position. And in the banking and financial ecosystem businesses, bonuses are common (and substantial) for those who are part of the decision making processes (which is governance). In the military, senior officers usually have personal staff, including "adjutants" that might accompany the senior officer from posting to posting, and which often informally help with family and personal needs. These and other examples abound, and they are all necessary for these powerful individuals to be more effective, but you must be careful not to break the law by abusing your perks or privilege.

Rule number two, is probably "Use it or lose it". Power hates a vacuum, and when you do not cash in and use your benefits according to the rules, you can end up being ignored by this ecosystem or it can be perceived as a weakness by your peers and lead to your loss of position within the ecosystem. Mind you, this last point can be difficult for the non-drinker who has the perk of unlimited liquor, or the politician who sticks to "the truth and nothing but the truth", but it can be done if the individual has information and is willing to use it. If a benefit is being unused by an individual, employees or family members might take advantage of the freely available perk, much as the chairman's spouse will borrow the image and authority of being powerful. Similar cases are the fraudulent use of a powerful person's name or identification, etc., undetected. But more important than the benefits for the rich and powerful, are the many benefits in this system for the resto of the people who interact with it.

Some benefits that are available are called "security safety nets" because they offer emergency or disaster assistance to individuals who qualify for it, or assist low income families with food or other needed resources. These are benefits that show up in the news media when they are abused, but in reality they build the wealth of the nation by allowing greater number of citizens and residents to overcome adversity and start producing individual wealth. Basically, if you are eligible for a benefit, that benefit will sooner or later get back to the government, so you really should use it. But you should also consider scholarships, grants, donations, specialized assistance, and even volunteers as a benefit of this ecosystem: Top colleges and universities fund the studies of top students that will increase their prestige; Top companies will offer internships to top candidates as an identification and selection process for new employees; public libraries and many colleges offer free access to learning materials that can be used to acquire saleable skills and knowledge, to mention just a few instances in which cashing in might not be through a public agency, but through a private or commercial entity. The interesting thing is that you must apply for these benefits, if you are to enjoy them.

Let me give fair warning: the danger of the governance and power ecosystem is that it can fool you into misusing or even ignoring rules from other systems. It is like going on an "all expenses paid trip", and overspending on gifts and personal expenses that are not covered. You are responsible for your actions, and in the governance and power system you can lose everything due to a serious mistake. For an innocuous example, not requesting a benefit formally at the right time could make it very difficult for you to receive the benefit later. These are called "eligibility windows", and they are like a mechanical warranty: useless after the "valid until" date has gone by. To cash in you really need to get the information before you need it and prepare to make a proper application.

Students are a very special case because most lack basic information on how to plan for college. For starters, public colleges might seem cheaper but when a good student applies to a top college with a rich endowment, that student can receive extensive financial aid that does not include loans. These "needs blind" colleges and universities offer extensive financial aid on a "first come, first serve" basis, so students should always apply for the financial aid as soon as they can. And they (and parents) should ASK QUESTIONS! One interesting situation is that of students whose parents saved in special "college funds accounts": these funds are included in the financial needs equations. The big advantage of having these college funds is the flexibility they offer the student who accumulates enough to pay the full bill at the college of his/her choice.

The third rule, which is critical for all of those entrepreneurs and innovators that are entering the world of governance and power, is to be compliant with all rules and regulations. Cashing in to the opportunities of new contracts, new technologies, new markets, etc., often requires legal advice as to not breaking any law, and though fortunes might be made by running the risk of getting caught, developed countries tend to block all of an individual's assets when they are accused of certain crimes. Compliance is like insurance: it seems expensive until the moment you need it.

Cashing in with compliance is basically represented in quicker approvals for permits, licenses, etc. and the ability to avoid government and powerful organizations from interfering with you. And, it opens up the possibility of getting other benefits that you may find you are eligible for.

In this sense, documentation and paperwork can offer benefits to everyone in that ecosystem: for example tax returns can prove eligibility for different forms of rebates, tax benefits, or financial aid of different types, and this applies to all sorts of specialized documentation that government offices have information on.

The fourth rule is more of a "best practices" recommendation, in that it is to focus on delayed gratification. Cash in legally by setting up income streams for after you are out of the position you held in the governance and power system. Acquire the skills and information, and wisdom hopefully, that will allow other income streams to flow naturally. This is the pathway expressly offered to USA armed services veterans, who may also receive retirement income if they qualify, but it is open to everyone who has perks and benefits available. Invest in your intellectual and personal development, make strategic long term investments, and use perks and benefits intelligently.

The classic Mark Twain novel **"The Prince and the Pauper"** is an interesting example of what happens when someone is moved into a new monetary setting. It might seem a foolish work of fiction, but Mark Twain was a master craftsman, and he knew human nature. The pauper was an outsider of almost all monetary activities and the prince was being trained in the government and power ecosystem. The novel is fun to read in and of itself, but it also holds some hints as to how power and government worked in the past.

To close this section, let me just remind you of an old "Reader's Digest" story: The father doctor gave advice to his son who had just taken a new job as a town physician in a remote rural area. The father told his son to buy a Cadillac before going to his new job. When the son objected, the father told him that if he showed up at his new job with the shiny luxury car, the town's people would understand that they were paying for his car, but wouldn't accuse him of overcharging them in order to buy it. The son followed the advice and continued accumulating wealth all of his life thanks to this critical life lesson. And, in the government and power ecosystem the lesson is not to let the rest of the population perceive that you are getting rich off of your position, which means getting rich off of their money, because they will get angry. Rags to riches stories are wonderful, but they can generate a lot of resentment.

CASH IN on good advice!

Specialized advisors, consultants, mentors, coaches, and such, are critical in every ecosystem, especially in the government and power ecosystems, because our 21st Century civilization has grown extremely complex and the corresponding monetary ecosystems are truly complex. To properly maximize your benefits and gains, you need good and informed advice before you cash in.

Most individuals learn good and bad lessons on the payments and commerce ecosystem through upbringing, media and basic education, but only those that are taught by successful communities within each ecosystem can feel confident of understanding how to cash in in that specific ecosystem. They can also assist in cashing in over time, which is a key element of banking and financial monetary gains, and they can help you avoid common mistakes which may cost you in the corresponding or even all ecosystems.

Free advice is usually available from government agencies, public libraries, specialized business associations, and more, but do not ignore paying a specialist if your decision could have huge costs or benefits: minimizing risk often requires investing in insurance or information. As you become conscious of moving within the three ecosystems, you will find many opportunities to benefit, and some of them will be very risky while others will be easy to make use of. Look before you leap is good advice here, and then ask questions and weigh the answers. Then, make your plan and definitely start to CASH IN!

VI. Conclusion

So, as we wrap up this simplified and highly irregular exploration of our monetary and value transfer global systems, let me just point out that at the time when Adam Smith wrote *The Wealth of Nations*, nations needed to accumulate value in tangible, fungible treasuries that could finance wars and respond to national emergencies. This is no longer the case, since the global network of government exchange created after the end of the Second World War and the creation of the United Nations is based on law and agreements, not physical assets. The new global economy now includes huge trading blocks and military industry organizations—highly criticized by libertarians and populist leaders—that set the stage for a sizeable reduction in the dependence of national assets for responding to unexpected needs. However, what has clearly increased is the need for ongoing national wealth creation, through the efforts of the populace: the opportunity for individuals to actively participate in the payment system and make use of consumer financial services, which are the doorway into modern banking and financial systems. These banking and financial systems, in turn, are the foundations for the governance and power ecosystem to thrive.

As I see the wealth of nations under this different perspective of ecosystems, it seems evident that **freedom is key to wealth creation**, and that the strength of the so-called *"cruel and inhuman"* capitalist system is precisely that it fosters more individual freedom than any other economic philosophy, by encouraging entrepreneurship and creative use of the financial system to stimulate wealth creation. Let us remember that in other financial systems the poor are usually excluded from education and opportunity and live a life of servitude or subsistence. In this sense, monopolies end up being anti-capitalist because they destroy individual opportunity and initiative through the monopoly's power and ability to control monetary flows and transactions. Similarly, the idealistic alternatives—given names such as communism, populism and socialism (which often lack a clear definition) soon turn into basic systems for redistributing power and channeling wealth to the new rulers. History shows us a few exceptions for every system that worked well thanks to honest and ethical leadership, until these leaders stepped down and new interests changed the nature of that specific political/economic system. Call it corruption, if you will, but I will simply call it a return to the feudal vision of accumulating treasure for yourself, and not for your people or nation.

For an individual to cash in on the benefits of each ecosystem, as explained here, is a productive process for increasing individual, community and national wealth, for it leverages the money creation possibilities of each ecosystem with the individual's skill and efforts.

As humanity transforms in the 21st Century, and global entrepreneurship creates new realities and new mechanisms for creating wealth, monitoring systems are also being established, and engineered to identify flows of value and illegal diversion of funds that reduce the nation's wealth. As boys and girls receive education and formerly excluded classes are incorporated into the national economy, nations are becoming more prosperous. And in the poorer nations, subsistence farming is slowly transforming itself into opportunities for wealth creation that these farmers access through technology and the now ubiquitous cell phone system. In addition, new technologies are making traditional precious metals less valuable in comparison to the rare elements that are used in modern electronics and that are imported from poorer nations. The education of women in these poor countries must be credited with part of this transformation, because these women become a resource and a form of wealth that acts against abuse and destruction in their communities.

As an advocate of the expansion of humanity into outer space in the near future, I believe these three ecosystems will reach out beyond our atmosphere. Yet, the control mechanisms will face the same problems that kings of old faced when they authorized explorers to find new wealth for the kingdom: it is impossible to really control someone who is out of your reach. At the beginning stages of human expansion beyond our planet's surface, wealth creation in outer space will probably follow the pattern of being taken "back home" in order to be converted into recognized and easily converted into riches, with many unintended and unplanned consequences. In the end, I suppose that technology and time will create a new monetary and economic reality specific to outer space. This could either be like the three ecosystems described here, or be something completely new, just like finance/banking and government transactions are now totally different from their historical origins. The 21st century renaissance—also called the Space Renaissance—truly promises great things for humanity; yet, even though it creates great opportunities for wealth generation, change will always be resisted by most individuals: it is human nature.

It seems evident that Humanity now faces new frontiers: the oceans, the frozen tundra, and outer space. Thanks to the continuous development of new technology that allows us to live in those places, each will offer even more opportunities for wealth creation. But recent history suggests it will not be governments who create the real wealth in these new frontiers: it will be the innovators, the people themselves. Those that concentrate and move wealth away from productive activities do not create wealth: they make money that does not bring life to the nation or the people. That is why I conclude that a nation's wealth is created by the ones that create, produce, work, pay, buy, cash in on benefits and ask for loans to finance their new ventures. These are the people who will always create new, lasting wealth for their nations, and it is my desire that you – the reader = are one of those individuals.

Bibliography

Daniel Berleant, *The Human Race to the Future: What Could Happen - and What to Do.*

Frank Fenwick McLeod, *The History of Fiat Money and Currency Inflation in New England from 1620 to 1789.*

Salim Ismail, *Exponential Organizations: Why new organizations are ten times better, faster, and cheaper than yours (and what to do about it).*

Robert T. Kiyosaki and Sharon L. Lechter, *Rich Dad, Poor Dad: What the rich teach their kids about money that the poor and middle class do not!*

Richard J. Maybury, *The Future of America: History Repeats (The Great Monetary Calamity Series Book 1).*

Richard J. Maybury, *Time to Bail Out? What to do with Your Money: The Bernanke Bomb (The Great Monetary Calamity Series, Book 2).*

James Rickards, *Currency Wars: The Making of the Next Global Crisis.*

Adam Smith, *The Wealth of Nations.*

Peter Watson, *Ideas: A History of Thought and Invention from Fire to Freud.*

Soto, Hernando de *"The Mystery of capital: why capitalism triumphs in the West and fails everywhere else."*

Ron Chernow, *"Alexander Hamilton"*

T. Harv Eker *"Secrets of the Millionaire Mind"*

Other sources

Association of Certified Anti-Money Laundering Specialists (ACAMS) articles and opinions, in LinkedIn.com and acams.org

http://europeanhistory.boisestate.edu/latemiddleages/banking/

Financial Action Task Force (FATF/GAFI), gafi.org

FinancialPlanning.com

EconoTimes.com

AmericanBanker.com

Treasury Management Network, in LinkedIn.com

FINTECH Circle, in LinkedIn.com

TED Talks:

How global crime networks work (2009), Journalist Misha Glenny
http://www.ted.com/talks/misha_glenny_investigates_global_crime_networks

What gives a dollar bill its value?, Doug Levinson
http://ed.ted.com/lessons/what-gives-a-dollar-bill-its-value-doug-levinson

Special Drawing Rights and the International Monetary Fund

Extracted from article in EconoTimes Aug. 25, 2015

"Special Drawing Rights" are an especially attractive condition that some currencies achieve in the IMF. But that does not mean that the SDR is a "global reserve currency" nor that having the country's money the SDR basket is the financial equivalent to being a permanent member of the U.N. Security Council. The SDR basket was created by the IMF in 1969 as a "supplemental reserve asset" to provide liquidity to countries facing balance of payments crises, allowing central banks to draw on these moneys (presently the U.S. dollar, the euro, the British pound, and the Japanese yen, with the possibility of including the Chinese RMB in 2016). Though it is a source of prestige, being a SDR-contributing country does not give much real power, since it is the IMF's Executive Board. Central banks, institutional investors, and speculators who decide what coin to hold and how SDR basket funds are used. In addition, the SDR basket is altogether worth under $300 billion, which is a drop in the bucket compared to the more than 11 trillion dollars held in global currency reserves in early 2015.

For all the SDR's inconsequence, the price China has to pay for the RMB to get into the basket is huge. Including China in the SDR basket will require that China further open its capital markets, which will not only create investment opportunities but also serve as a massive disciplinary tool to further push China to improve its economic performance and the way it governs its economy. Being an SDR member will also further embed China in the current global order, giving it a greater stake in providing public goods to the rest of the community and improving the system, not working against it.

To be accepted for inclusion in the basket, a currency must be both "widely used" and "freely usable." China can easily check the first box, as it is the world's largest exporter, and at least a quarter of China's trade is conducted in RMB. According to the Society for Worldwide Interbank Financial Telecommunication, or SWIFT, the renminbi is now the fifth-most widely used currency in international transactions. It's the "freely usable" part that's the rub; currency flows in and out of China beyond trade and foreign direct investment are highly circumscribed. Only a small group of about 300 "qualified foreign institutional investors" have been approved to buy into China's securities markets; their $100 billion in investments accounts for less than 3 percent of China's stock and bond markets. As a result of these constraints, the RMB likely accounts for less than 5 percent of turnover in global foreign exchange markets, and central banks outside China hold very little RMB in their official reserves. The People's Bank of China estimated in June that overseas central bank holdings were only the equivalent of $107 billion, and a substantial portion of that amount is held by the Hong Kong monetary authority. The Middle Kingdom's currency is peripheral to central banks.

China will also have to open up the two-way currency door much more widely if its currency is to be included. That's good for the non-Chinese financial community, which would gain far greater access to China's equity and debt markets, and could attract more Chinese capital abroad.

But even gradual reform poses a huge risk for China. Greater financial openness may be just the market medicine China needs to become more efficient and ensure sustained growth over the next few decades. But it also makes China more vulnerable to sudden capital inflows and outflows, which could trigger a crisis if investors either pour money into China, generating inflation, or conversely, lose faith in the Chinese economy, depriving it of oxygen.*

Fast Forward to 2017, comment by Manuel Perez:

The Chinese financial ecosystem has had a rough time in the first half of 2017, with its stock market in turmoil and many Chinese investors moving a portion of their wealth into foreign currencies, foreign assets, Bitcoin and other cryptocurrency. Part of the difficulties is government policy, and others seem to be investments in infrastructure that have yet to bring about commercial expansion. Interestingly enough, China's Government level ecosystem seems to be expanding, with international loans among third world countries that are creating much good will and influence, which counteracts its huge US debt holdings that probably make it uneasy.

The Chinese government has clear plans for military expansion at sea and in space, and they are offering small countries an opportunity to join them in their expansion and the economic motor they have set up in their first two monetary ecosystems. My personal thought is that they might have already set up payments and financial ecosystems that are temporarily too large, as they plan to grow in accordance with their expansion in the governance ecosystem. But there is a risk that this could never come about due to lack of trust. If other countries and Chinese investors do not trust the central Chinese government, the potential and preparations of the past 30 years could still fall apart.

NYC, July 2017

www.ingramcontent.com/pod-product-compliance
Lightning Source LLC
Chambersburg PA
CBHW070240230526
45470CB00002B/462